UNBROKEN LOVE

Overcoming Sexual Dysfunction in a Christian Marriage

RACHEL LOUISE

Copyright © 2021 by Rachel Louise

All rights reserved. No part of this book may be used or reproduced by any means, graphic, electronic or mechanical, including photocopying, recording, taping or by any information storage retrieval system, without the written permission of the author, except in the case of brief quotations embodied in reviews.

Paperback ISBN 978-1-945169-57-1
eBook ISBN 978-1-945169-59-5

Published by
Mercy & Moxie
an imprint of
Orison Publishers, Inc.
PO Box 188, Grantham, PA 17027
www.OrisonPublishers.com

Unless otherwise indicated, all Scripture quotations are taken from THE HOLY BIBLE, NEW INTERNATIONAL VERSION. Copyright © 1973, 1978, 1984 by International Bible Society. Used by permission. All rights reserved worldwide.

This book is dedicated to all Christian women and partners who are affected by sexual pain disorders. It can be difficult to share such a private pain with others, and it took over twelve years for this book to be written. I battled with God about sharing this personal pain—I felt embarrassed about telling such intimate details about myself—but after realizing how many women and couples are struggling, I knew this story had to be told. So I used a pen name. I hope and pray that my story will bring some comfort for you to know that you are never alone. Please find a message from me at the following link: https://www.youtube.com/watch?v=AhEWyTlJau4.

Table of Contents

Introduction: "It's Not Your Fault" — Exposing the Secrets in My Closet ix

Section One: Roots and Seeds: Childhood xix
Chapter One: A Religious Upbringing 1
Chapter Two: Till Sex Do Us Part? 21
Chapter Three: David–Lost Era of Innocence 31
Chapter Four: David–Addiction 41

Section Two: Shoots and Leaves: Marriage 55
Chapter Five: Pain in Spain 57
Chapter Six: My Vagina Has What? 71
Chapter Seven: Newlywed, Constant Dread 85
Chapter Eight: The Valley of the Dry Bones 101
Chapter Nine: Dr. Frank Gets Frank 121
Chapter Ten: North American Victories 133
Chapter Eleven: Hopes and Dreams 143
Chapter Twelve: A Big Sting in the Tail 155

Section Three: Flowers 169
Chapter Thirteen: A New Journey *With David's Perspective* 171
Chapter Fourteen: Growing a Family *With David's Perspective* 179
Chapter Fifteen: Financially Blessed and Restored 189
Chapter Sixteen: Bringing Down the Walls 195

A Letter to the Reader 201
Appendix 1: Template Letters for Family Doctor/Spiritual Leaders 203
Appendix 2: Quotations of Encouragement 207

Acknowledgments

I would like to thank my husband, who has stood with me while writing this book and has offered encouragement to share our story. Thank you to my family and our parents for allowing us to share sensitive information from our childhoods. This information will allow readers to see how my condition developed over years of receiving messages surrounding sex that were not always positive.

I also believe that it is important for readers to get to know our characters and the backdrop that led up to our marriage. This book started off being a collection of private journal entries that enabled me to capture what was happening and helped me process my emotions and beliefs. It then developed into a story, and chapters were developed. As the book started to take shape, it was further developed by editors David Rose, Sandra Byrd and Barbara Kois, whom I cannot thank enough for their input.

I thank God that even though I carried much shame with my disorder, He allowed me to experience this pain so that I can now support women and their partners who feel alone in a similar situation. I thank my two beautiful children for being patient and allowing me time to write this story. I know that some days it seemed like I was glued to my laptop.

I hope and pray this story will help women and their partners see they are not facing this fight alone, that it can be overcome, and that they have not been forgotten by God.

> Sincerely,
> Rachel

INTRODUCTION

"It's Not Your Fault"
Exposing the Secrets in My Closet

"Above all, be the heroine of your life, not the victim." —Nora Ephron

A psychologist once asked me why I believed that my experience of vaginismus was somehow my fault. I supplied many answers that day, with tears streaming down my face, including my belief that I should be normal, like everyone else, so that David should not have to put up with it. The psychologist sat and listened to all my expressions of guilt, shame and low self-esteem.

"Do you think," he asked me, "that a person should feel guilty about the impact their illness has on their partner if they have been paralyzed from the waist down and they have difficulty with having sex? Or what about the lady who has had cancer, has lost both of her breasts, and is having trouble being intimate? Do you think she should feel guilty?"

The psychologist sat back and patiently awaited my answer.

"That's different," I replied. "They have an illness that they have no control over!"

The psychologist paused for a second.

"Is it different?" he asked me. "If you had control over your situation, would you not be choosing to engage in a sexual relationship?"

Silence seemed to fill the room as I reflected on what he had said.

"Like many people who suffer with illness and disorders," he continued, "you also have a problem that you have no control over at this point in time. For some reason, the muscles in your vagina have decided to tense and spasm every time that you attempt to have sex. So why do you feel guilty about something that you, at present, have no control over?"

Sharing this story, a story that has brought ridicule, shame, loss and disconnection from the safe and secure world of the church I was raised in by my parents, is one of the most difficult decisions I have had to make. Although I have always known that this story was given to me for a reason and that the purpose of God sending my husband and me through these tribulations was so that it could benefit others in some way, I could not see how my story was relevant to others.

When I was diagnosed with this condition, I was informed that only 1 percent of the women around the world struggle with vaginismus, now referred to as Genito Pelvic Pain/Penetration Disorder by the DSM-5 (Diagnostic and Statistical Manual of Mental Disorders). I recently learned that at least 10 percent of women are now estimated to experience painful intercourse and two in every one thousand women are estimated to experience primary vaginismus. Many live with fear of being ridiculed, mocked and shamed.

Vaginismus is defined as a tightening of the muscles that occurs when something tries to penetrate the vagina. This could be something as small as a Q-tip or from sexual intercourse. Often, the woman will respond by tensing her thighs and raising her buttocks off the bed. Many women state that when they attempt to place something in the vagina, it feels like they are hitting a brick wall.

After ongoing prayer and reflection, I began to realize that although this story is intended for the two in every thousand women who have vaginismus, others can profit from the insights gained by the experiences of my husband and me. This story is much more than a story about one couple's journey of living with a sexual disorder. This story is about how many individuals and couples attend church gatherings while hiding a secret that they feel they can share with no one—whatever that secret might be.

Living with a sexual pain disorder for more than ten years has allowed both my husband and me to experience the negative effects of having no one to provide us with support and the devastating effects that hiding such suffering and distress had on our Christian ministry. Sadly, our situation was so serious that it ate away at both of our identities and self-esteem. Every day that we remained in a Christian leadership position, we felt fake and unable to be our authentic selves due to the fear of becoming rejected and discredited within the same.

Like many others, I had been taught that it was not okay to have unresolved psychological issues such as depression, anxiety or panic because they were not of God. But God never promised anyone that life would be easy, and some of us will at some point in our lives fall victim to physical complaints, while others will be more prone to emotional or psychological disturbances. Having the latter does not make an individual any weaker; illness in all shapes and forms, including addictions, are part of life, and suffering with any illness or disorder does not make a person unworthy of acceptance. John 9:3 says, "'Neither this man nor his parents sinned,' said Jesus, 'but this happened so that the work of God might be displayed in his life.'"

Some leaders within Christian churches have indicated that being ill is in some way a punishment from God, a physical display of a person's sin. Although illness is a part of life and it is no secret that all of us are mortal and will one day die, I do agree that God did not intend for us to live our lives sick. He said to the man who lay unable to walk at the side of the pool, "'Get up! Pick up your mat and walk.' At once the man was cured; he picked up his mat and walked" (John 5:8–9).

Clearly, God does not intend for us to live our lives sick and does want us to be well. There were many times during my struggles that I cried out to God to cure me, but He chose to allow me to endure my disorder. If God stepped into every situation and took away the struggles, the suffering and the painful times, how would we learn? On reflection, I see that my time living with my disorder allowed me to address a lot of underlying values and beliefs I had about myself and those around me, and on reflection, it allowed me to grow into a much better person.

I remember someone sharing an analogy of a rough stone and how it doesn't just become shiny. It is bounced around, and the rough edges must be smoothed down, and then after much work and effort from the creator, it becomes a beautiful precious stone that many people admire.

But every time I began to think about sharing this personal and humiliating story, I started to feel a wave of nausea and panic. *What will my friends and family think about me? How will sharing my story of pain and suffering really benefit people? No one will be interested in my story—how will it even be relevant to them if it's about a journey of suffering with a sexual pain disorder? What if people ridicule me? How will I become a credible person if they see how much psychological distress I have had in my life?* I began to fear that my story would make me a lesser person who, in the eyes of society, was a person broken and beyond repair. My ideal of being able to help people would be gone, because they would see that I had struggled and that I was weak and didn't have it all together. Pious Christians would start to pity the fact that God had not answered my prayer and would believe that it was due to my lack of faith for healing.

As I began to listen to the negative thoughts that flooded my mind about attempting to share my story, a quiet thought caught my attention. *God didn't just give you this affliction and this pain without reason. What would be the point of that? God gave you this story so that you could make others aware that there may be individuals around them living with psychological distress and to comfort those who are experiencing distress and who falsely believe they are less as a result.*

Jesus Himself freely chose to accept death on a cross so that each one of us could have eternal life. John 3:16 states, "For God so loved the world that he gave his one and only Son, that whoever believes in him shall not perish but have eternal life." He chose to give Himself to death in a way that opened Him up to being mocked, ridiculed and disrespected, but He did it because He knew that by doing so, He was serving a greater purpose than protecting His own life, pride and reputation.

If you were to disclose your innermost fears, what would you say? Maybe your fear, anxiety or phobia is something that you do not wish other people to know about. If your neighbor or friend found out what fears, anxieties or crazy scary phobias live hidden away deep down in your closet, maybe you would be ashamed and embarrassed. You might wonder how they could even begin to understand or accept the daily fears you are experiencing when you cannot even understand them yourself.

Fear and anxiety can present in many ways. My fear began as a fear that no woman ever wants to discuss, as it is a fear that most of society would not understand—sexual dysfunction. How could I share a fear with family and friends regarding an area of life that is so personal and private and taboo to discuss? Talking about sexual fears is not something that you can just blurt out to your close friend over dinner, or even after one or four glasses of wine.

I also battled a fear of taking medication because I was afraid I would have a severe allergic reaction to any medication I took. Eventually, this fear grew, and I found myself starting to experience difficulties with eating particular foods. My avoidance of food often prevented me from visiting friends' houses for meals, and some became offended when I asked what was on the menu. Informing a friend that you cannot eat around fifteen different foods becomes embarrassing when they begin to figure out that you are not experiencing an allergy at all but rather a deep intense fear that an allergic reaction could occur and you will die a sudden death.

My fears and anxieties continued to morph out of control to the point that I was unable to drive anywhere alone. If I did try to go out alone, I would start to feel a sense of impending doom and I was unable to get my breath. I felt like I had to tell myself to breathe, and if I didn't tell myself to breathe, I would suddenly stop. I felt like the world around me was starting to spin, and pins and needles moved up my hands, and my body felt like ice. There was a sense of dissociation, whereby I felt like I was close to leaving my body and detaching from the world around me, and this caused me to panic because I started to believe I was dying.

Suddenly, I became aware that my heart was racing, my breathing was deep, and a surge of energy was buzzing through my body that made me want to flee the situation. I often found that I needed to turn around and drive home so that I could feel a sense of safety again.

The act of having sex, which most people find occurs naturally, feels impossible to a woman who has perceived threats and fears, whether unconscious or conscious, around sex. Some women struggle with sexual pain caused by post-traumatic stress disorder (PTSD), which causes their bodies to perceive a further threat after being subjected to an actual threat, such as rape or abuse. But the fear of having sex does not always come from experiencing abuse as a child or adult. There are many other causes, both physical and emotional.

For example, a fear of sex can often be built up from the constant messages a woman receives regarding sex before marriage and the shame that comes along with that. I remember the strong messages about sex before marriage being bad and the shame that would have been created if I had engaged in the act before marriage. Having no experience with sex, the buildup to the wedding created much anxiety about what sexual intercourse would be like.

I remember David (my husband) being sent for an HIV test because of his high-risk background with intravenous drug use and being concerned about his exposure to sexual infections. This lifestyle was alien to me as a devout Christian, and the anxiety that built around these thoughts of contamination was possibly a contributing factor to the development of my vaginismus.

As unusual as it sounds, as a young lady who had grown up in the Christian church, my fear was that I was about to engage in a sexual act that I had always been informed was sinful and wrong. For those who choose not to wait until marriage, an individual's first experience of sex remains a private and intimate time that occurs and passes without anyone else necessarily knowing. Like me, I am sure many women who save themselves for marriage can relate to the thoughts that their first experience of sex does not feel private. Before sex has even occurred, expectations have already begun that the act that consummates the marriage will occur on the wedding night. Looking back, David and I had already built up expectations for that night, and I felt aware that family and friends would know I would be having sex, an act that had remained forbidden and wrong until now. With these thoughts and expectations, I felt extreme pressure to complete the deed on my wedding night. It was almost as if there was no escape, and it seemed that it would be unacceptable for me to say I was not ready to complete the full act of sex on my wedding night. The reasons for my vaginismus would be found to be physical too.

Wearing a mask of happiness to hide a shameful disorder while continuing to carry out daily activities sometimes feels like the easier option, rather than being forthright and honest about your hidden struggles. Others may cope by shutting themselves away from the world and are left with a sense of frustration, loneliness and desperation for circumstances to change.

Living with a sexual dysfunction for twenty years is no laughing matter. It is a devastating and lonely disorder that steals all the joy that should be experienced by everyone. I want everyone to have that joy, which is why I am telling my story.

I have been blessed to have a husband like David, who refuses to give up on our relationship, sharing the pain of the anxiety, phobias and fears that I have experienced daily. A common view is that such partners are stupid and should end the relationship. Like many, I had begged David over and over to leave me and find happiness with someone else. Thankfully, many amazing partners choose to remain with their loved one through some of the most difficult and lowest points of their partner's life.

True love is unconditional, and I have learned that within marriage or civil partnership, there are happy memories, devasting points and times, and boredom. Every partnership comes across challenges that leave the couple with a decision about whether they should stay or leave. There are situations that warrant an individual leaving a marriage, especially if abuse is taking place within that relationship. There are also many situations where couples give up too quickly and the commitment to each other fails at the first point of challenge. I am so glad we did not give up.

Pain and suffering can be overcome, even when the situation seems impossible. I hope sharing this story will help to raise awareness of the devastation that psychological distress about sexual dysfunction can cause.

No one observing from the outside would ever have imagined that David and I had a problem. This book shares the experience of living day-to-day life with much more than a sexual pain disorder. Although our story is one of sexual fear and pain, it will be fully relatable to many couples and individuals battling through other challenging life issues that threaten their partnership and their family's security and happiness.

As I listened to that psychologist point out that this was not my fault, I slowly began to see his point. I left his office that day feeling as if part of the weight had been lifted from my shoulders. I then began to reflect on how my condition had impacted David and how my inability to have sex had unexpectedly deeply affected his life. My pain and devastation had become David's pain too.

After eleven years of struggling with vaginismus, I had connected via email with other women from around the world who were also suffering from the disorder. Some I had found via YouTube, others through professional contacts and some on vaginismus chat sites. All the women were looking for the same things: connection, answers and a cure. Like so many women suffering from the condition, I was still in a personal state of crisis. How could I ever help others if I could not even help myself?

That night, I began to realize that I was the only person who could sit in the driver's seat when it came to dealing with my situation. I was the only one who had the power to bring about real change. I knew that I still needed the support and input of professionals, who could offer appropriate treatments, advice and support. However, I realized that they would never be able to resolve my issues if I did not act as the driving force for my own recovery.

I needed to know where I was going and who I needed to accompany me on my journey, so that I could reach my destination. Being a registered nurse by profession, I had witnessed many individuals who had not taken responsibility for their health. Even though they had been diagnosed with a condition, they would continue the same habits that had caused their condition in the first place—for example, the individual who had a heart attack but even after a near-death experience continued to eat poorly and live a sedentary lifestyle. I also witnessed individuals who accepted their condition but chose not to let it beat them. They would research everything, and they would do everything possible to change the habits and beliefs they had been taught, in a hope that it would change their situation. I started my nurse training at the age of twenty-four and at that time I was still the assistant pastor's wife. I had worked as a care assistant for many years, and I felt that training to be a nurse would allow me to do a job in which I could support people who were facing crisis. After working in many different areas of nursing, I eventually found a job in the intensive care unit in a busy oil and gas city in Canada. I would spend my days monitoring patients and providing treatments as their lives balanced between life and death. This job had many nights where I had time alone to think about life, especially when I constantly witnessed how precious and short life is and how tragedy can just strike without warning. As I sat caring for a patient into the early hours of the morning, I realized that I needed to take control of my own situation if I were to serve as a catalyst for change for other women struggling with vaginismus. As I soon discovered, the process of change can be painful, but also possible.

My name is Rachel, my husband is David, and this is our story.

SECTION ONE

Roots and Seeds: Childhood

CHAPTER ONE
A Religious Upbringing

"Return to the root and you will find the meaning." —Sengcan

Early Seeds and Sex Education

I grew up in a religious Pentecostal home, where any kind of sexual behavior prior to marriage was believed to be sinful and wrong. Sex before marriage was almost considered to be a dangerous act. Our beliefs had taught me and my family that sex before marriage was wrong, but after marriage it is an act that is to be enjoyed fully. I was never really informed that sex could be fun, permissible or exciting as it was not a topic that was easily discussed. When it was discussed, it was more about ensuring that I remained abstinent until I got married. So sex was never talked about in a lighthearted or fun way. I was never encouraged to use tampons or given instructions on how to insert them, since my mother had been taught that tampons could be dangerous if they were left in too long. As she had been taught the dangers of toxic shock syndrome, that also concerned me. I thus developed a fear that tampons could become lost in the vagina.

My mother, through no fault of her own, was always overly concerned regarding toxic shock syndrome with tampons. She simply taught her daughter what she herself had learned, so using sanitary pads was deemed to be safer. My few attempts to insert tampons ended in failure, since I had no idea how to even work it. I would often place them at the entrance to my vagina but would then be too fearful to even try to ease them inside. I began to believe the lie that the tampon would enter my vagina and never be seen again.

Looking back, I can see that many seemingly small issues, built up over a lifetime, can contribute to anxieties, phobias and the disorders they bring or enhance. To be free of them, I would need to go back to the earliest days and understand where the seeds had been planted.

Sex was not a subject my family discussed openly or in a positive way. On the rare occasions that it was talked about, sex was usually spoken of negatively, since there was great fear that I might engage in sex before marriage and bring shame upon my family. TV shows that featured any sexual content were quickly switched to another channel. Whenever I asked questions about sex, the situation was always uncomfortable and awkward, so I never really got to understand what sex really involved or what it was all about.

Even at the age of eighteen, I was naive about sex. I understood the basics, but my sexual education was mostly based on what I had learned from advice columns or from my friends at college. My parents were loving parents who wanted the best for their children, but when it came to discussing sex, I did not feel a sense of permission to openly talk about my fears and concerns. Because sex was off the agenda before marriage, it was an unspoken rule that it was not something that needed to be discussed.

Unexpected Adventure

My parents, Don and Julie, had only been married for a couple of months when they realized that they were expecting their first child—me. Mom was twenty-one years old when she gave birth to me at the northern City Hospital in the United Kingdom in May 1977, and they named me Rachel. I was a shy and introverted child who got along with everyone. I was a happy child who enchanted everyone I met with my mischievous smile. With bobbed black hair, blue eyes and pale skin, I was the child who was often spoiled with toffee sweets given to me by old people at the church.

A Religious Upbringing

I was the sort of child who loved riding on the back of my dad's motorbike. You would also find me helping Dad at the local Christian youth club, where I sold pop and chocolate from the shop that my dad set up every Friday night. I enjoyed the company of my family, and we were close.

When I arrived at college, my friends would ask me to go nightclubbing with them. Nightclubs, drinking and hooking up with boys was something that had never been encouraged in my family. I remember asking my parents if I could go. I sat and spoke with Dad about the choices I could make, and the decision was left to me.

Although I wanted the freedom, part of me was worried about being so vulnerable. What if something went wrong? Whom could I trust if my family were not around? I had heard about the bad things that happened in nightclubs and had been taught they were not safe places. I knew the expectations of my parents, and nightclubbing, drinking and meeting non-Christian boys was not what they had expected from me. Although my parents shared their expectations, they never imposed restrictions upon me. I was encouraged to make choices and learn from my mistakes.

My mom was a devout Christian woman who worked as a part-time cashier in a small shop at the local university. She was a good mother to me and my brother Nathanial, and she was also quiet in nature.

They had many success stories of helping foster children placed within our home who had been damaged by abuse and had to learn to trust again. I remember one eighteen-month-old boy whose mother came to take back custody. When his mother picked him up and walked away to her car, he reached out his arms and screamed for my mom. As I stood on the step next to my mom waving good-bye to yet another foster child, I realized how blessed I was to call her Mom. Another older boy with behavioral challenges ran away from his home, and he was found hiding in a camper in our backyard. He was another of the many disadvantaged children who found safety and love within our family and did not want to leave.

My parents fostered lots of children throughout the early years of my life. One day, Mom and Dad decided that they wanted to leave the city where I was born to manage a children's home fifty miles north of the city.

Permission to Enter

It was August, and my brother, Nathanial, and I had been playing outside on our bikes. Nathanial used to love riding as fast as he could up and down the street, trying to prove to me that he was the best rider. When we returned home to have dinner that night, both Nathanial and I could sense that something was weighing heavily on the minds of our parents.

"Sit down, kids," said Dad. "We have something that we want to ask you both. Your mom and I have been given the opportunity to run a children's home, which means that we would be looking after not just one or two children, but maybe as many as six to eight children at a time. Now, it means that we would all have to move to a bigger house that is out in the countryside. If we decide to take this job, then you would both need to leave your school and friends behind."

As I quickly glanced over at Nathanial, I could clearly see excitement on his face about the adventure that lay ahead. "When would we go?" he asked. "Can we see the place?" Nathanial asked lots of questions, and his excitement seemed to grow with every question.

"Rachel, what do you think?" Dad asked. "Would you be willing to move away from your school and friends?"

"Well, I would miss my best friend, Rebekah," I replied.

I had never been away from Rebekah, and we had always experienced everything together. However, I could clearly see how much this new opportunity meant to my parents. As a family, we all believed that we had been called by God to do this work.

A couple of months later, we were all packing up our belongings and saying good-bye to friends and family. The new house was only an hour away, but to me, it felt an awfully long way from home.

When I arrived at my new home, I stared at the big black-and-white house situated in the beautiful open countryside. The building had previously been used to nurse tuberculosis patients after the war.

After moving into the incredibly old, vacant, and frankly, haunted-looking house, I became quite obsessed about things being clean. My bedroom had a strong musty smell, and the dirty bright-yellow walls had to be washed down before I could be persuaded to move in. There was also an old hospital bed with a dirty striped hospital mattress in the corner of my small bedroom, which added to the strange atmosphere of the place that was now my home.

A neighbor told me that there were witches hiding out in the nearby forest who prayed to Satan that the home would be closed. When I heard that, my imagination ran wild, and I began to think that I was seeing ghosts in my bedroom.

I now wonder if my fear of germs at that early age was an indication that I might be someone who would be susceptible to a disorder like vaginismus later in life. My phobias expanded into having an extreme fear of dying, which usually involved dreading severe allergic reactions.

For example, when I first got married, I was deeply concerned that I would be allergic to David's sperm. It has been suggested by some scholars that some women with sexual pain disorders may even suffer with a defensive mechanism that causes the woman to feel a sense of disgust. A concern about being contaminated could even cause the symptoms of sexual pain disorders such as vaginismus in some women. It is a question I still ask myself to this day—if my fear of something entering my body contributed to the physical aspect of my muscles clenching when penetration was attempted. I was unable to swallow tablets and feared injections, which both required permission to allow something to enter my body.

Growing Shame
Eventually, the home was opened, and children began to move in. Most of the time there were about four or five children staying with us, so I did not have many days alone with my parents. The foster children had often been physically, sexually and emotionally abused. Having so many children around did take away one-to-one time I had with my parents, and there were times that I craved more time alone with them. I sometimes felt like I was constantly competing with other children for their attention, but deep down I knew this was not because we were not important. I was aware that there were other children who had never experienced love and safety and seemed to need my parents more than I did, so my emotional needs could not always come first. I took on a role of assisting my parents with caring for the other children. I would often sit and help them with homework or counsel them when they were sad or angry. I

fell in line with my parents' expectations, as I knew that I would take precious time away from caring for children with needs if I started to act out. It was not until my late teen years that I felt a permission to act out with my behavior.

When I look back to my childhood, I see that my parents were strict and had many expectations for how I should behave and be, and these expectations were another seed that was planted that I believe made me more susceptible to vaginismus. Being a parent myself now, I realize that unconsciously we are often unaware of the expectations we place on our children and the messages we send. I still battle with placing expectations upon myself and relate my ongoing need to reach the expectations of others to my vaginismus.

Looking back, it seems like I created many expectations that had to be met before I had even entered the bedroom. One expectation I had was that my first sexual experience was going to be magical, and everything would be perfect. I failed to recognize that sex does not always go according to plan the first time around. It takes practice, and to become the best lover, you must learn about the needs of your partner. Rarely do first-time sexual experiences turn out exactly as a couple had hoped.

When my wedding night did not go according to plan, it was catastrophic, and I stacked up thoughts of everything that could possibly go wrong the next time around. My mind-set became fixated on everything that was wrong, rather than focusing on what could go right. My thoughts raced with worry, and I replayed the pain and the failures in the bedroom until the moment I found myself back in the bedroom trying again.

My parents were very skilled with the children, who all truly became part of our family. Some were like brothers and sisters to me; they would often share their deepest and darkest secrets. I cannot recall conversations with foster children about their abuse stories, but I do remember an incident with a foster boy that may have contributed to the shame I felt about sex.

I was around thirteen, and one of my foster brothers and I were hanging out in the camper in our backyard. We never used the trailer for camping, but we loved to go and sit in it and pretend we lived there. It had a small living area, a kitchen and a bedroom. At some point, my foster brother persuaded a girl from my school who was visiting me to pretend to have sex. As I sat on the sofa, they hid under a blanket and were making suggestive noises and laughing.

Without any warning, the camper door swung open, and there stood my mom, who appeared alarmed at the scene she had discovered. As my mom interrogated me about what she had found, I remember the deep sense of alarm, shame and guilt that I felt even though I had not participated in anything that she had observed.

Looking back, this situation most likely planted a seed of shame about sex that I had been completely unaware of. I remember the sense of guilt and shame I felt even though I had not participated, as if I had failed my parents' expectations.

For seven years, I lived in that old black-and-white wooden house with my family, until my parents once again approached Nathanial and me for yet another serious conversation. However, this time it was to inform us that we were being made homeless.

Losing Control and Trust
Nathanial was distraught. "Why do we have to move again?" he asked. "I like this place, Dad!" Nathanial slumped down into the nearest chair and emitted an exasperated sigh.

"We like it here too," Dad told him, "but this time it hasn't been our decision to move. The churches that are funding the home have said that they cannot afford to keep it open anymore. They are selling the house to a radio station. I am so sorry, kids. I know you have both enjoyed living here."

"But where are we going to go, Dad?" I asked, while poking the roaring warm fire coming from our open fireplace in the living room. "You and Mom won't have jobs, and where will all the children go?"

"They'll go back into foster-care homes, Rachel," Mom replied. "It's sad, but there is nothing we can do to stop this from happening. The churches have made their decision, and it's in their hands now. As for your dad and me, well, no, we don't have jobs, and that is a big concern. But we don't want you and Nathanial to worry about that. We'll probably get subsidized housing, and the government will have to support us for a while."

"What about the savings from selling the house, Dad?" I asked. "There must be some money saved from the sale of the house after we moved out here. We could use that money."

Dad sat very quietly before he replied. "The money from the house is gone, Rachel," he admitted. "The money we received from the church for running the home was nowhere near enough for us to survive on as a family. So that money from the house has been paying the bills that we were unable to afford with our wages. It's all gone, Rachel. We have nothing left."

One by one, the foster children said good-bye to our family. There was a great deal of confusion and many tears. While the radio station and the churches put contracts into motion, they allowed our family to remain at the home and my parents took care of the house until the official date occurred for possession, which was a period of around two years. Once the date for possession of the house was agreed, our family had six weeks for the local council to find us a home. A few weeks before we left, Dad got the keys to the place we would call home for the next few years. When I walked into our latest home, I was shocked. The walls were covered in graffiti, the house had broken windows, and fleas seemed to be everywhere. The doors were all hanging off their hinges, and the entire house was filthy. Thankfully, Dad was able to work on making our new home adequate for our family to live in before the day came for us to move. Although the council house was not perfect, Dad had at least managed to get the flea problem under control and cover the broken windows in the kitchen. Once the place officially closed and the day came for our family to move, Dad drove our family toward our newly acquired accommodation.

This childhood experience left me with a great sense of being out of control. I had been brought up to trust the leaders of the church. I had always been taught that they were there to protect and guide us, yet I had been left feeling like they had let my family down. It was not until many years later that I was informed that the churches had allowed our family to remain at the house for a few years prior to our departure. As a teenager, my perception of the situation was extremely different. All I saw was the stress my parents were experiencing while worrying about having nowhere to go due to the council not intervening until we were threatened with immediate eviction. I saw the worried looks on my parents' faces and heard the heated telephone calls asking for help and witnessed the inadequate house that was deemed acceptable for our family to reside in. Sadly, the church had no option but to serve a quick eviction notice so that our family could be offered emergency accommodation. Such circumstances taught me to try to maintain a sense of control over my life and to be careful about whom I trusted in the future. I believe that my fear of losing control became a contributing factor in my development of vaginismus.

My parents argued frequently, as Dad was not adjusting well to the experience of being unemployed and living in a rundown home. Eventually, he was able to paint the hallway in order to hide the graffiti on the walls, and later, he was able to decorate the house with the help of our extended family. When we left the children's home, thankfully I had already left school and was attending my first years of college, but Nathanial was having to be driven to and from school daily to complete his final exams. We spent around eighteen months at this property until our family was to move again.

After all his hard work, Dad was offered another job, which included a house on-site. So once again, we packed up our belongings and moved. It sometimes felt as if we were never given long enough to truly settle anywhere. A house was never really a home, since it always seemed to become only a temporary arrangement. However, things became more stable once our family made our last move, to a small city. Although my family had been made homeless and I had felt forgotten by the church, this was not a hurt that our family carried. It was not until many years later while battling vaginismus that all the hurt feelings about the church came tumbling back. When I was unable to continually reach all the high expectations of the church, my self-esteem became damaged.

Seeking Approval

One hot summer evening, my dad and I enjoyed the beautiful sunshine as we sat in the garden looking at a map of the world together.

"I've always liked the idea of a vacation in Canada," I said.

Dad took a sip of his ice water and smiled at me. "Canada!" he exclaimed. "It gets extremely cold out there. What about somewhere like Australia? That's much warmer!"

"Australia would be nice too," I replied, after considering what my dad had said about the weather, "but I've always wanted to visit Canada. There just seems to be something special about the place."

"Well, you'd better start saving now then, Rachel," Mom shouted from the kitchen. "A flight to Canada will cost you a lot of money."

My mom knew that I probably would save the money and go, since she knew I was someone who dreamed a lot. Once I put my mind to something, my mom knew that there would be no stopping me. My last adventure had been to Belfast, Northern Ireland, which I had completed by myself after getting in touch with a church there. Even though the area was still unsettled, I had already decided to go there and work at a youth center on Shankhill Road. Mom had worried about my safety, but she knew that I was adventurous and did not want to stand in my way. Mom most likely realized it was only a matter of time before I would come home and drop the bombshell about Canada.

"Three months!" she exclaimed when I came home one day with the news. "I thought you said you wanted to go on vacation to Canada, not go there for three months!"

"Well, it's not really a vacation, Mom," I explained. "I'd be going as part of a Christian team, with a preacher who visits Canada all the time."

"Do we know this man, Rachel?" asked Dad, sounding somewhat suspicious. "I'm not sure I like the idea of you going away to a foreign country with a man we've never met."

"He's a famous preacher, Dad," I replied. "You can talk with him if you want. He usually works in Israel, and he visits Africa too. He's seen healings and he's an amazing man of God. Please, Dad! This is my chance to visit Canada!"

This was not the first time I had gone away, and it wouldn't be the last. I was good at putting my case forward and could see that my parents were slowly coming around to the idea. Although I was eighteen and in the eyes of the law I did not need their permission, my parents were still very much in control of the decisions I made, as I always had a deep need to please them and gain their approval.

Without their permission, I likely would not have visited Canada. They did not need to beat me with wooden sticks to control me. Just a disappointed look from one of them or realizing I had not met their expectations, and I would retreat. This sense of needing permission from my family is yet another unconscious, deep-rooted behavior that may have contributed to my personal development of vaginismus.

"Well, why three months, Rachel?" asked Dad. "And what exactly would you be doing out in Canada?"

"He wants me to sing, Dad!" I replied. "I'd be singing in churches in Vancouver, Calgary and Winnipeg and in lots of small towns too."

"You already sing in the churches here," said Mom, "so why do you have to go all the way to Canada? Who'll take care of you out there?"

But my mind was already made up. I was eighteen years old now, so my mom fully understood that the final decision was mine. She knew she had to accept that I was a dreamer and was always going to be doing something.

"I'll be staying with families from the churches out there, Mom," I reassured her. "It'll be fine, I promise."

I spent three months in Canada, where I sang at many churches, went door to door telling people about God, and ran programs for children and youth in the church. Once again, I was involved in religious activities and surrounded by Christian leaders I respected. I never once got into any trouble.

There were no secret love affairs or drinking alcohol. Nobody ever had to tell me to be good. If I perceived that I was doing something wrong, I would correct my behavior before anyone could see that I had accidently fallen out of line.

My seeking of approval and needing to meet my parents' and church expectations began to become a need in all of my relationships. If I failed to impress my boss or made a mistake, I would be the first person to beat myself over the head with a wooden stick, figuratively speaking. Conflict was never an issue with friends, as I never fought against what they wanted.

I loved Canada and the people I met. There were still many rules and expectations from the Canadian church that further shaped my need for approval. Whether I was back home in the UK or traveling in Canada or Ireland, it seemed that there were always rigid expectations that I needed to meet for me to feel accepted. I remember one afternoon my traveling partner was flicking through the Canadian TV for something to watch. As he flicked through the channels, one of the channels was displaying some sexual content. Before he could flick to the next channel, the father of the host family began to shout at us and informed us of his disappointment that we would watch such content while staying in his house. I remember trying to plead our innocence but being told not to lie. Yet again I was left feeling ashamed and guilty.

When I returned home, I missed Canada so much that I cried for days. Being away from my family had given me a sense of independence and allowed me to venture out of my shell.

Seeking Security

As I lay on my bed at my parents' house, I began to seriously consider what I wanted out of life. I had always wanted to be a social worker and help children, just like my parents had done. However, I was not sure now if this was the path I should take. I recalled what the woman had said to me during my interview for the social work program in Oxford, United Kingdom.

"Rachel, we would love to have you enroll in our social work course, but when I look at your history, I see that your whole life has been social work."

Maybe she was right. My whole life had involved being surrounded by children from abusive backgrounds. From the time I was a small child right up to the age of seventeen, I had been around children who had been physically, emotionally and sexually abused. Maybe venturing into the field of social work at such a young age would be a bad idea?

As I lay on my bed, I thought about what I had been told in Canada.

"You should come here and live with us, Rachel! You can take a job as my nanny and go to the Pentecostal Bible school and do your degree."

The woman I had been staying with in Canada had four amazing children, and I had become close to all of them in the three months we had been together. She had driven me out to the Bible school to see if she could encourage me to register for the theology program. However, the school was extremely strict, and they allowed no makeup, no interaction with the opposite sex, and no drinking of alcohol. I began to feel that living under such strict rules would not only be unhealthy, but also not much fun. Still, there was the prospect that I might be able to consider a theological college in England.

At this point in my life, I honestly believed that attending Bible school in the United Kingdom was the next logical step. It never once crossed my mind back then that I was simply running straight into the arms of another security provider, namely the church, which once again had expectations that I must meet.

Although there was a sense of control and expectation with my family, I always felt secure and loved. I knew the rules well and what was expected of me. The church was a place where I never seemed to reach the expectations that were set. But something deep inside of me seemed to have a need to be accepted by the church. Instead of choosing to study a secular degree, I decided to study a degree at a Bible school where I would spend the next few years. I remember my first introductory evening at the college. The pastor who had dedicated me into the faith as a child was speaking that night to all the new students. I remember him acknowledging me and asking why I had decided to attend Bible school rather than secular school.

"Why Bible school, Rachel?" he asked as he sat back in his chair, waiting for an answer.

I nervously glanced around the room, seeing that all eyes were on me waiting for a response.

"Well, I want to serve God and sing around different churches and be an evangelist." I smiled back at him, proud of my response.

"Rachel, just because you attend Bible school doesn't mean that you will get invited to sing at churches. What about a career? You should be thinking about your future. It is unlikely that you will ever make it just singing around churches. Bible school is for those that want to serve as pastors, not someone who just wants to sing."

I sat back in my chair, feeling like all the excitement about Bible school had already been sucked out of me before I had even begun. Had I made the right decision? Maybe he was right! Maybe I should have trained as a social worker instead of chasing the church and continually trying to meet their expectations.

Although I could sing, I was never chosen to lead worship at Bible school and was often overlooked when opportunities arose, due to my quiet nature. There was always someone more talented, more beautiful and more charismatic than I was. It began to seem like my childhood pastor's words had been right, and I started to wonder why I had chosen the path of Bible college. I started to believe the self-limiting story that I was not good enough, and this was before I had even faced the trial of vaginismus, which in years to come planted even more seeds of feeling inadequate. Although I had always had difficulty placing tampons from the time I was a young teen, it never occurred to me at this point in my life that I had something wrong. I was unaware that vaginismus existed because back in the 1980s, it was not a topic of conversation that would be openly discussed and was not a condition that was widely publicized. Not being able to insert a tampon was one of the first red flags for vaginismus that I had failed to recognize.

Rather than truly allowing myself to explore what I genuinely wanted out of life, I chose to remain in the only "bubble" I was familiar with—church and religion. I tried to hold on to a sense of control in my life by sticking to what I knew best. However, my world was about to change. Attending Bible school in the UK was where I would begin to lose all sense of control in my life.

As I placed my belongings in the closet, I could hear the faint hustle and bustle of the other new students as they returned to their rooms. A few people introduced themselves, although it was clear that many had already quickly formed relationships. On the first morning of classes, I walked into the classroom and sat down alone in a corner and opened my textbook. As I glanced around, all I could see were little groups of people talking among themselves.

Why did I have to be late? I thought. *If only I had gotten here on time for the welcome meeting, maybe I would have made some friends.*

A few minutes after the class had begun, a young blond-haired girl quietly crept into the class and scanned the room for a convenient place to sit. As she glanced in my direction, one of the girls from the group opposite me waved, inviting the blond girl to come and sit with them. As my heart started to sink with thoughts of having no friends for the next three years, suddenly the chair next to me was pulled back as the blond girl sat down beside me.

"Hi, my name's Ruth," she said as she quickly pulled out her textbooks and tried to keep up with the lesson.

From that day on, Ruth became my best friend. We went everywhere together and often loved to play pranks on the other students and faculty members.

Meeting David

One afternoon shortly thereafter, I sat in my communication-skills class preparing to deliver a talk about homelessness. It was a topic I had always been passionate about and while studying, I volunteered at a local homeless shelter. Deeply lost in my own thoughts, I was suddenly startled by a hand placed on my shoulder.

"Hi, is this seat taken?"

A tall skinny-looking man in his mid twenties with terrible fashion sense was staring at me, waiting patiently for my answer. He did not fit the usual stereotype of a Bible school student, which was well dressed, from a middle-to-upper-class family, and well spoken. In fact, he looked like he had not received an adequate meal in months, his clothes did not match, and he spoke quite abruptly with his heavy Glaswegian accent. His clothes looked to be secondhand and well worn. His hair was not cut into the latest style either. His dark hair had a rather big cowlick, and his sideburns were so long that he looked like he was living in the 1970s rather than the 1990s. I had met him briefly before on a few occasions but had not really noticed him until now.

"Yes!" I blurted out. "I mean, no, it's not taken. You can sit here."

I could not help but notice his smile, which was beaming from one side of his face to the other as he spoke.

"I'm David, by the way," he said, still smiling.

"Yes, I know your name," I replied. "It's good to meet you *again*, David."

I quickly looked down and continued to work on finalizing my speech. It was already finished, but I could feel myself beginning to feel a little flustered by David's presence. As I sat next to him in communication class, I found myself unable to look him in the eyes. The last time we had met we were so rude to each other, and now, here was David, smiling at me.

I had spoken with David a few days before, but neither of us had introduced ourselves because we were too busy arguing. David was the leader of our dishwashing team, where each student had to contribute to the upkeep of the college by participating in cleaning duties. I was normally eager to help, but I was confined to bed, sick with tonsillitis.

I had recently returned from visiting the doctor, and I had been told that I should rest. I was in bed when there was a sudden loud and demanding knock on the door. As I got out of bed and tried to make myself presentable, the knocking became more insistent.

"Okay, okay," I protested, frantically trying to dress myself to open the door. "Just a minute."

I had barely gotten the door open when an angry Scottish man, who I later knew as David, started yelling at me. "You're supposed to be on wash-up duty this evening! You may think it's okay to shirk off and hide out in your bedroom when the mood takes you, but I don't!"

At the time, I had barely any idea who David was, but I was very annoyed with him.

"You know," I hoarsely replied, barely able to raise my voice, "maybe if you had asked first if there is a reason why I wasn't at washing-up duty, you'd realize that I am sick! So now that you know I am sick, can you leave me alone and stop shouting at me?"

I slammed the door on a stunned David.

Back in the classroom, I did everything in my power to avoid eye contact with him. However, when David got up to complete his speech, I found that I could not help but snatch a few brief glances at him. When he began to talk about a subject close to his heart, I found that I could no longer avoid eye contact.

As I listened to David's strong Scottish accent and heard of his passion for helping those struggling with drug addiction, I was spellbound. As David continued to share with the class about how he had been physically abused, homeless and had battled his own demons with drug addiction, I found myself warming to him. I had never met a young man who intrigued me so much and who seemed to be as passionate as I was about helping the disadvantaged.

As I sat in the class listening intently, I was unaware that David was just as intrigued about my passion for the disadvantaged as I was about his. Both David and I had experienced disadvantage in our lives and we both knew how challenging life could be. It was not always possible to remain in a positive mind-set when there seemed to be no end to the suffering being faced. Part of what drew David and me together was being surrounded by many from an advantaged background, and both of us feeling like misfits.

We had experienced hardships that were alien to many around us, so from the very beginning we had a strong, unbreakable connection that to this day has always remained. From that day forward, David and I made excuses to talk to each other. David would often walk into town with me or pass by my room and stop for coffee. We both found that we could talk effortlessly for hours on end, and we both knew that we had found a connection that neither of us had initially expected. When I had decided to attend Bible college, I dreamed of becoming a Christian singer who would encourage people. When I met David and we both found that we had a heart for those who were suffering, it seemed that both of us wanted to enter the Christian ministry to make a difference in people's lives.

We inspired each other, and I found myself longing to spend more and more time with David. Neither of us realized that spending so much time together was starting to upset certain people at the school. For example, David's ex-girlfriend attended the Bible school and happened to be my roommate.

"You can't trust a guy who wears white socks, Rachel," she confidently asserted, "especially with black shoes."

David's ex-girlfriend had just heard the news that David was showing a lot of interest in me. She tried saying everything she could to try to put me off him. However, I refused to listen to her negative comments.

Confessions over Coffee

One day, David asked me to go shopping with him in the small, rural village that was not far from the college. In a quaint French café, I sat opposite him nervously sipping my cup of tea, wondering if he liked me as much as I liked him. David flashed me a mischievous smile.

"Do you think it's ever right to tell a lie?" he asked, smiling as he continued to sip his tea.

I assumed he wanted to engage in a philosophical discussion and began debating the positive and negative elements involved in telling a lie. "Well," I replied, "I guess it depends on why you're telling a lie, doesn't it? If a psycho with a gun asks me which way an innocent victim went, I am definitely going to lie to save that person from being killed. However, if I tell a lie with no good reason, then I believe it's wrong."

My heart raced as David smiled and stared at me inquisitively across the table.

"So," he said, "here's the question then. If it is wrong to tell a lie, then how do you feel about me?"

Completely caught off guard, I began to splutter and cough, almost choking on my tea. As I looked at David, I could see him laughing at my shocked response. I realized that he had tricked me into revealing whether I had feelings for him. My face began to feel flushed and hot.

As I looked around the café, I noticed that other people were also looking at me and grinning. It felt as if everyone had stopped what they were doing, eagerly awaiting my reply.

"Well, err…" I stammered, "I guess if I were to give you an honest answer, I would say that I like you, a lot. So, what about you, how do you feel?"

"I like you too, Rachel," he replied with a shy smile, "and I've wanted to ask you out for a while, but I guess I wasn't sure if you felt the same way. So, I had to think of a way to tactfully ask you."

From that day on, David and I were inseparable. We spent most of our time together, visiting with other couples, eating takeout fish and chips and Indian curries. With each passing day, we fell deeper in love, and it was not long before we knew that we would always be together. When my parents first met David, I remember their concern over his past addictions and past experiences of being homeless. Even before David came on the scene, I felt the need to seek their approval for boyfriends I chose. David often confided that he felt he never reached my parents' expectations and was not good enough.

When we were forced to spend three months apart, both David and I realized that absence really did make the heart grow fonder. I had become sick with a very severe case of glandular fever and had to return to my parents' home to recover. However, I always looked forward to the long phone calls, the romantic letters and David's visits, after his long two-hour bus rides to visit me at my parents' home. I still treasure one letter that David sent to me while we were apart.

Hi Rachel!

It's yours truly. I'm sorry that I haven't written, but it's been quite difficult to find the time up here. It was great to speak to you on the phone. I can't wait to see you on the 22nd! Tonight, I wrote up my sermon for Sunday night and sat and watched Inspector Morse! Well, we haven't got long to go until our church practical experiences have finished. It will all soon be over, and then you'll get one week's vacation!!! I am prattling on here, as I don't know what to say, we covered it all on the phone!! I really do miss you, Rachel. It feels strange not being able to see you. Still, it won't be long now, only nine days to go. Like I said, I want the biggest, best, most passionate, romantic, long kiss whenever I see you! (Not in front of your parents though!!) By the time you get this letter, it will be Friday or Saturday. I'm away on Monday morning, so please write back to me at the college address. Rachel, you're special, you're cute, you're whacky and you're "one cool chick." I love you and I'm praying for you.

David xxx
P.S. I miss your crazy noises and faces!!

I have the letter to this day. It made me realize that like other couples, David and I were in love and were happy. We could not have known that we would soon be faced with the biggest trial of our lives together.

Seed for Thought
"A farmer went out to sow his seed, as he was scattering the seed, some fell along the path, and the birds came and ate it up. Some fell on rocky places, where it did not have much soil. It sprang up quickly, because the soil was shallow. But when the sun came up, the plants were scorched, and they were withered because they had no root. Other seed fell among the thorns, which grew up and choked the plants. Still other seed fell on good soil, where it produced a crop—a hundred, sixty or thirty times what was sown" (Matthew 13:3b–9).

CHAPTER TWO

Till Sex Do Us Part?

"Worry does not empty tomorrow of its sorrow, it empties today of its strength." —Corrie ten Boom

David booked a table at an upscale Italian restaurant and then traveled to my home and knocked on my parents' door. As I opened it, I could see by the look on his face that he thought I looked beautiful. I was dressed in my little black dress and high heels and had spent so long putting my makeup on that it looked very professional. With my long black hair down and perfectly straightened, I was ready for our special night to begin. I noticed that David was not wearing his jeans. This was certainly unusual, since I could not remember ever seeing David not wearing his jeans.

As we walked to the restaurant, hand in hand, we were both excited about what the evening might bring. David and I both knew that we wanted to be together, and I was convinced that it was only a matter of time before David asked me to marry him. The fact that David was not dressed casually was my first clue that this might be the night he would propose. As I sat eating my pasta in candlelight, David suddenly pulled out a ring.

"Marry me, Rachel?" he blurted out.

He didn't get down on one knee, like they do in romantic movies.

David was so nervous I was surprised that he didn't drop the ring. While trying to clear my mouth of food, I found myself staring down in awe at the beautiful diamond engagement ring.

"Yes, yes, of course I'll marry you!" I excitedly screeched with tears in my eyes as I tried to gulp down the rest of the pasta in my mouth.

David placed the ring on my finger, and I was so proud to show it to my parents when we got home. Although Mom and Dad were happy for me, they had a few concerns about David's history, which I could certainly understand. However, they respected my decision and the wedding plans eventually commenced.

Planning Ahead

We were both in the second year of our degree course, so we barely had enough money to spare to plan for our special day. One afternoon, while sitting reading her newspaper, my mom noticed an advertisement. It was for a wedding dress that had never been worn before, and it was for sale for eighty British pounds (about $110 US). Apparently, the woman who had purchased the dress had decided not to get married after all. The wedding dress was beautiful, and it fit me perfectly. It was pure white and had a long hand-embroidered train. Everything seemed to be going so well, and all the wedding plans were finally coming together. Now we just had to decide on a honeymoon destination.

"What about going to Greece?" I suggested. "I've always wanted to go to Greece."

After studying the cost of the trip outlined in the numerous travel brochures, David looked extremely disappointed.

"We can't afford these places, Rachel," he said. "They're too expensive."

I desperately tried to think of ways I could raise the money but soon realized that it was not going to happen.

"There are some Christian travel deals in Spain," Dad suggested as he showed David the brochure he had been reading. "It's a coach group tour, but your mom and I have always enjoyed them."

My dad had always been able to locate good deals and was well known for being able to find practical solutions to problems.

"I guess the prices are pretty reasonable," I agreed. "What do you think, David?"

"Well," he replied, "I think your dad's right, Rachel. We can't really afford any of the other options, so I think this is all we can do right now."

The location that interested us both was in Pineda de Mar in northern Spain.

"Yeah, I agree," I whispered, while winking mischievously at David, "but I'm not sure that I want lots of people around us all the time."

Overhearing my comment, my dad continued to try and sell us his idea of a group tour.

"Well, I'm sure you won't be expected to stay with the group all the time," he told us. "Anyway, it might be nice to meet some new friends."

Finally, a decision was made, and we booked our travel to Spain.

As the countdown to the special day began, I had started to feel nervous about my wedding night. I was still a virgin, as I had decided to save myself for marriage. As a devout Christian, I had always believed that this was the right thing to do. As you can imagine, the weeks leading up to the wedding day were stressful, with so many things to do to get everything prepared, but I also grew more and more anxious about the wedding night. I assumed that this was a normal reaction, especially since, as a virgin, I really had no idea what to expect.

Although I had wanted to talk about my fears and apprehensions about sex, I felt far too embarrassed to raise the subject with my friends. Sex was not really a subject that I openly talked about with anyone. Whenever I had attempted to engage in conversations about sex with my mom, it always felt very awkward. Mom and I had never seriously sat down and discussed such things. I knew that my mom had tried to do her best to prepare me.

Very soon, I was going to be placed in a situation I had never experienced before. I knew I needed to do everything I could do to obtain the information I needed to prepare myself for my wedding night.

My preparation merely consisted of listening to the dramatic accounts of my friends, and it seemed as if their sexual experiences were not dissimilar to those found in the advice columns and help pages of magazines. Some of the stories I heard were frightening and traumatic. I vividly recalled accounts of women bleeding uncontrollably after sex, or a story about a couple that had ended up in the emergency room after the woman's boyfriend had gotten stuck inside of her. Other girls complained of the excruciating pain they experienced when their virginity was taken. I became terrified and was completely unprepared for my wedding night.

The Big Day

I awoke early on the morning of my wedding day to the sound of my Uncle Philip's loud knock on the bedroom door. My uncle had been selected to drive me to my hairdresser's appointment in Derby City Centre. After being pampered by the hair stylist, I returned to my aunt's house, where a busy household of family and friends greeted me. I felt so special that day, like I was the most important person in the entire world.

The makeup artist had arrived, and she took me to my Aunt Shelly's bedroom for some privacy, so that she could work on making me appear more beautiful than I actually was. As I felt the stroke of the makeup brushes against my face, I could hear the faint voices and laughter of family and friends downstairs.

How I wished that I were downstairs too, enjoying all the fun. After everyone had left for the church, I suddenly became aware of the surrounding silence. Only my dad remained with me.

"Is the car here yet, Dad?" I asked him, as I anxiously peered out of Aunt Shelly's window. "I'm going to be late!"

"I think you'll find that most brides are late for their wedding, Rachel," my dad assured me. "That's the way it's meant to be."

Desperately trying to distract myself, I began to pace around the house in my wedding dress. I clutched my flowers tightly, trying to stop myself from worrying that the car was never going to arrive. As I glanced over at my dad, I could see that he looked as nervous as I did. He was doing his best to keep me calm, but he probably knew that it was not working.

"Here's the car now," Dad finally announced with relief in his voice.

When we finally arrived at the church, I could see the hundreds of guests who were already seated, eagerly awaiting my arrival. I began to feel quite lightheaded, and when I began to walk down the aisle, I quickened my pace. Dad calmly attempted to slow me down, to ensure that I was in time with the music, but it must have felt as if he were struggling in a tug-of-war.

I quickly glanced around the church and immediately noticed that everything looked perfect. I could not have dreamed of a better wedding. I even managed to say the word *matrimony* without stuttering. Finally, the day had arrived where David and I could exchange our vows and start a new life together.

As I walked down the aisle with my dad by my side, I felt as if I was at the beginning of my very own fairy-tale or was on a spectacular Hollywood movie set. I almost felt as if I needed to pinch myself, just as a reminder that it was not only a dream. I had finally found the man I wanted to spend the rest of my life with, my true soul mate. When I finally reached the front of the church, I felt almost hypnotized as I happily gazed into David's eyes. As he grinned from ear to ear, David's eyes held my gaze, and I instantly sensed how much he loved me. When I turned toward the vicar to begin the ceremony, I felt David quickly grab hold of my hand. As I discreetly glanced back toward his intense gaze, David leaned in closer to me.

"I love you, Rachel," he whispered.

The wedding ceremony went more smoothly than I could ever have imagined. Everyone had gone to so much effort to make our day special and memorable. Friends and family were present and both of our mothers were in tears by the end of the ceremony. Everything was perfect. I was on top of the world and I felt that nothing could ever bring me back down to earth.

Something Is Wrong

After the evening buffet had finished, everyone returned home. My mom and dad drove David and me to our hotel. The honeymoon suite was beautiful, with a big TV, a king-size bed and a huge Jacuzzi bathtub. I felt like a princess with my tiara still glued to my head, considering all the hairspray it had taken to keep it there. After opening the champagne, David and I quickly undressed and dived straight into the hot and relaxing Jacuzzi bath.

"Ah, that feels so good," said David, as he sat in the Jacuzzi, sipping his champagne.

As we lay entwined together in the water, we passionately kissed between the many glasses of champagne. Feeling very relaxed after our soak in the Jacuzzi, David made his way to the bedroom.

I swiftly slipped into a beautiful white basque camisole with stockings and the super high-heeled shoes I had worn for the wedding. As I checked myself in the mirror, I was pleasantly surprised at how amazingly good I looked.

When I entered the bedroom, David started to smile and obviously thought his new wife was sexy. The next thing I knew, we were kissing intensely. It felt so good not to have to hold back. Finally, we were allowed to express how much we loved each other. I had been patiently waiting my whole life for this night to arrive. At last, I had found my soul mate, and David and I were finally free to make love. Then, as things began to become more passionate, I shouted out loud.

"Arghhh! It hurts! Stop!"

David immediately stopped what he was doing. He looked a little shocked, to say the least, and tried to reassure me that it was natural to initially feel a little discomfort. He patiently tried again to penetrate me.

"Arghhh! It hurts so badly!" I exclaimed. "I can't! Stop! Please stop!"

David quickly withdrew from me with a look of utter confusion on his face.

"It hurts, David!" I confessed in total despair, as I sat upright in bed. "Surely it's not meant to be this painful. What's wrong with me?"

I had felt as if knives were searing through my vagina with an unbearable burning sensation every time David had attempted to penetrate me.

"It feels like I'm too small down there, David," I told him, "as if there isn't enough room."

David tried to reassure me, and we tried again and again, but on each occasion, it was the same. Every time we tried to have sex, it felt like we were hitting a brick wall. After numerous attempts, David decided to call it a night and made the decision that we would wait until we arrived in Spain.

It had already been an exceptionally long day. David and I were both extremely tired and slightly drunk from the champagne. David had made plans for the next day, and we were traveling to stay with his sister, Raylene, and her partner in Kent, in the southeast of England. From Raylene's house, we would take the bus to Spain.

My dream of a happy fairy-tale wedding day had unexpectedly turned into a hellish nightmare. As we both silently lay in bed, I was completely stunned and unbelievably upset at what was happening to me. From that night on, I was constantly asking myself, "What's wrong with me?" Our wedding night should have been the best night of our lives, an experience filled with happy memories that we could both treasure. Instead, we were left feeling alone, confused and embarrassed.

Living in Shame
When I imagined my wedding night, I thought we would experience a special feeling of intimacy that couples talk about feeling when they awake after a night of passion and romance, or that slightly awkward feeling over morning breakfast after such a night. I imagined holding hands and having uncontrollable smiles and the warm, glowing feeling people seem to talk about the morning after.

David and I had awoken to a buffet breakfast the next morning. However, there were no warm feelings or uncontrollable smiles. Instead, we felt only devastation and humiliation. The special moment we had both been waiting for had been ruined. Throughout the long awkward silence over breakfast, we somehow managed to communicate how we both felt and openly shared our thoughts and confusion. After finishing breakfast, we were both feeling more positive, so we decided to put our wedding night disaster out of our thoughts.

"Come on, babe, cheer up!" David said, holding me close to him. "We have our whole honeymoon to put this right. It's going to be okay, I promise."

Every time I tried to speak, I found myself crying. I didn't want to cry, so instead, I said nothing. As David eagerly walked out of the hotel to meet his sister, Raylene, and her partner, I choked back the tears and put on the mask of happiness that I would learn to wear very well. In the car traveling down to Kent with Raylene and her partner, I began to experience an overwhelming feeling of inadequacy and shame.

What if David tells his sister? I thought. *Raylene would surely tell David to leave me and find someone else, wouldn't she?*

Overcome by negative thoughts, I tried to remain focused on holding back the tears. I knew that crying would bring so much relief, but at the same time it would draw attention to my shameful situation.

No one can ever find out about this, I decided.

I glanced over toward David and I wondered what he was thinking.

What if he thinks he's made a mistake marrying me? I thought. *Oh, God, please don't let him want to annul our marriage!*

As I sat quietly in the car, I found myself starting to think about all the worst things that could happen. *Why did this have to happen to us? Why did we have to experience this devastating problem?*

I ran through one scenario after another in my head, speculating just how I would tell everyone why David had annulled our marriage. I imagined myself trying to explain my shameful situation to the leaders of the church or to my parents and my extended family. I could vividly picture the deep disappointment on their faces. I knew that I would be perceived as damaged goods. How could I ever be considered of any worth in the eyes of the church again? I imagined David's parents reproaching me too.

"How could you let this happen, Rachel?" David's mother would demand. "You must have known that you had a problem!"

There are no words that can describe the emptiness, shock, disbelief and shame I was feeling. It was as though all my dreams and hopes had suddenly disappeared. All my confidence and the very core of my identity had been violently ripped away. I no longer had a clear future mapped out in front of me.

For the first time in my life, I could no longer imagine myself as a mother, a wife or a good Christian woman. David had shared his own hopes that everything would be okay once we arrived in Spain. However, I had an awful feeling that this was a far more serious situation than simple wedding night nerves.

I found myself looking enviously at other women around me, wishing I were normal, like them. Tears started to fall down my cheeks. I quickly wiped my face as I looked out of the car, pulling my hair across my face to disguise my tears.

How can I even call myself a woman anymore? I thought. *I'm nothing more than a freak!*

The song "I'm Not a Girl, Not Yet a Woman" often made me cry when I heard the words, "I'm not a girl, but not yet a woman." That was how I felt. I no longer considered myself a child, but I could not bring myself to acknowledge that I was a woman. Whenever I tried to think of myself as a woman, I felt like a fake, a liar and a freak of nature. I honestly believed that I was the only woman in the world who could not have sex. How I wished for a friend I could confide in. If only there were someone who could understand my pain. However, I was about to find out that the journey of vaginismus was a very lonely one indeed. It would be years before I realized that there were thousands of women experiencing the same heartache and pain as I.

David and I arrived at the bus station and said our good-byes to Raylene and her partner. As we boarded the bus to Spain, Raylene began to cry, but she explained that these were tears of joy.

"I'm just so glad for you, David," she said. "I've spent such a long time wishing for you to be happy."

Please, God, I prayed, *please, will You sort this mess out? David has already escaped a life of crisis, and I can't bear the thought of causing him more suffering; not after all he's already come through.*

The bus finally arrived in Spain, and I knew in my heart that the trip might not be the beginning but rather the end of our marriage.

Seed for Thought
"'For I know the plans I have for you,' declares the Lord, 'plans to prosper you and not to harm you, plans to give you a hope and a future'" (Jeremiah 29:11).

CHAPTER THREE

David–
Lost Era of Innocence

"The only thing worse than being blind is having sight but no vision." —Helen Keller

Introduction to David
You may wonder why knowing David's story before we got married is important. His story shows how much pain and suffering he had already experienced and escaped before he met me. Knowing the battles that David had already fought and how God had turned his life around further filled me with guilt when I failed to be the wife that I felt he expected me to be. It led to further doubts about God's existence and why He would allow such a devastation to occur. David had already fought so hard to escape his life of drugs and homelessness and now he was faced with feeling trapped in a marriage that seemed doomed to failure. Before we delve into David's past, it is important to acknowledge that the past is the past and the future is very different. David has written an introduction below to introduce these next two chapters.

David: People can change. It is amazing to hear the powerful stories from people all across the world—men, women, boys and girls; those who are rich and those who are not; those who are religious and those who are not; those who are black and those who are white; those who are

heterosexual, homosexual and all other individuals with characteristics that mark their identity and diversity. The common unifying theme that I wish to emphasize is that people can, and do, experience amazing changes in their lives, irrespective of their personal idiosyncrasies and diversity. But it doesn't come cheap—it comes at a price. It may cost our commitment, time, friendships or acquaintances. It may even cost us money.

Before I launch into a brief recollection of personal experiences that give a snapshot of my life, it is important to understand that things are very different now in comparison to how things used to be. The personal conduct and perceptions of myself and my family have undergone drastic changes, for the good. My parents are now both Christians who have undergone amazing changes in their lives. They continue to be married and are very different people from how they used to be all those years ago. Where we were once estranged with regard to interpersonal connection, we now maintain regular telephone contact at least two times every week. Unfortunately, geographical distance between us places limits upon the regularity of our personal visits, but we do try to visit each other when we can. So, although we are not in the same location, we now share a closeness that was never there in my childhood. My parents now reach out to others and offer lots of wisdom and practical help. My sister has also undergone many changes in her life throughout the years and spends her time helping others with innumerable physical and psychological ailments in her career as an osteopath. We are also in touch with each other on a regular basis.

My intentions of contributing to this book are to simply reveal parts of my life in order to extend consolation and hope to any reader who may relate to the content. I trust that readers will be inspired by the journey of change, and as a registered mental health nurse, I welcome anyone who may wish to seek us out for personal support with matters relating to mental/psychological health, addiction issues and the marital issues that characterize the larger percentage of this book. Always remember that it would be unwise to label and define people on the basis of their past behavior, because people can and do truly change. That includes you. Do you believe it?

I, David, was born in 1971 and grew up in Glasgow in Scotland, raised by a policeman father and a mom who was a housewife. My older sister, Raylene, and I spent our early years in a Victorian tenement flat in Glasgow, whose ceilings were decorated with beautiful white Victorian cove molding and large, plaster floral centerpieces.

The dwellings of Glasgow were old buildings with sturdy spiral staircases that were ideal for children who enjoyed sliding down the winding bannisters. I remember the musky smell of tomcats in the "close," the tiled corridor-like entrance to the building where just about every cat in the entire neighborhood would spray its scents in order to stake out its feline territory. The smell of the cats and the fumes from the nearby diesel locomotives on the railway lines were not uncharacteristic of a street in good old "Glesca," the local slang term for Glasgow.

I was a mischievous kid back in the early 1970s and remember listening to The Eagles, T. Rex and Led Zeppelin on the radio during the hot summers. Mom would often find evidence of my mischief—squeezed toothpaste all over the carpets or cheese missing from fridge raids at two o'clock in the morning. If she were quick enough, she might even have caught me throwing as many porcelain ornaments, vases, pictures and toys out of the windows as I possibly could.

To this day, I am unsure whether my behavior was compatible with my developmental stage, or whether I was reacting to thoughts and feelings that were generated in the home environment. However, there were no repercussions for me getting up to mischief at that age. But I do remember being unable to get out of my room in the mornings, even when I attempted to turn the door handle. I am not sure if the door was locked or if I couldn't get a grip on the handle. I was only a kid.

Lying Low
At the age of almost five, I attended my first school. It was a nice school, but I hated the bully who was about two years older than me. The bully's name was Mark, and he used to walk up to me on the playground and whack the palms of his hands against both of my ears with a hard clap. I bounced around the playground alone most of the time to avoid my stalker.

When I returned home from school, I often occupied myself alone there too. My sister, Raylene, also maintained a low profile, since our father, Hamish, believed that children should be seen and not heard.

Consequently, Raylene and I both learned very quickly to keep out of our dad's way. No matter where I was, I learned to be wary.

One morning, I awoke from a deep sleep to find that I had wet my bed yet again. I knew that I would be in serious trouble when Dad found out. After I got dressed, I quickly removed the soiled bedding and quietly made my way down to the washing machine in a small room beside the kitchen. If I could just get the sheets into the machine, I knew that Mom would wash them, hopefully without telling Dad what had happened. As I crept down the hall with my wet sheets, I heard the faint echoes of the radio and the rustling of Dad's newspaper from the kitchen. Paralyzed with fear, I stood holding the sheets tightly, wondering how I could pass the half-open door to the kitchen where Dad sat.

If Dad finds out that I have wet the bed again, I'll be in so much trouble, I thought. As I turned around to make my way back to my room, I heard Dad start walking toward the kitchen door.

"Son, what are you doing?" Hamish asked as he glared at me.

I slowly turned around to face Dad. I knew that there was no point in lying, because Dad always found out.

"You've wet the bed again, haven't you?" Hamish asked, with his piercing eyes glaring with anger. "I'm tired of this! If you won't stop wetting the bed, then your mother and I are going to have to send you away to a children's home!"

As I stood crying in the kitchen doorway, Dad pulled out a black garbage bag and started to fill it with my clothes. I ran into the kitchen where I saw my sister, Raylene, quietly standing in the corner, crying. Mom stood with her hands on her hips to convey that she agreed with Dad.

"I'm sorry, Dad! I won't do it again!" I pleaded. "I'm sorry!"

"This has to stop now! I am sick of you and you sister wetting the bed! If either of you do it again, we will send you away!" shouted Dad.

However, I did wet the bed again, many times, and on each occasion, I felt the disapproval of Dad and often cried. They didn't send me away, so it must have been a tactic to try to shock me to stop wetting the bed.

Family Atmosphere

By the midseventies, I became more aware of the "atmosphere" in the family home, which had undoubtedly contributed to my anxiety and bed-wetting. My earliest recollection is of one late afternoon when Dad was out at work. Dad didn't want Mom going out or seeing any other people without him, so the curtains were closed as Mom, Raylene and I sat in the front room watching TV. It was the only time we all got to watch the programs we enjoyed, because Dad always watched the news on different television channels and negatively criticized anything that we wanted to watch. Anyway, there was an unexpected knock at the door and when Mom answered it, her friend Karen stood there.

"Hello, Dorothy," she said. "I'm taking Robert to the fairground and I wondered if you and the kids wanted to join us?"

There was a long pause before Mom replied. As she turned away from the door, I could see the look of fear in her eyes. Her uncertainty was obvious. I had witnessed this look of fear on my mother's face on many occasions. I knew that Dad would disapprove of her taking us to the fairground, since Dad didn't like Mom going out without him. Although Dad's disapproval usually resulted in lots of shouting, intimidating behavior and sometimes physical slaps, the fear of Dad finding out never stopped me from pleading with Mom to let us visit the fairground.

"Please, Mom, can we go?" I said, as I started to put on my jacket.

"Well, okay," Mom replied, "not for long, though, because your dad will be back home soon."

At the fair, I ran from ride to ride with Raylene and screamed with laughter while waving excitedly to Mom, as the rides whirled quickly past her. Stevie Wonder music was playing loudly through large speakers, and the song was "Sir Duke." Each time the ride swept us past the crowd of people where Mom stood watching, I could see the anxiety and fear that clouded her smile and that she desperately tried to hide from us. I knew she was not having the slightest bit of fun, but in my innocence, I didn't fully understand. As the other moms smiled and waved at their children, I watched my mom constantly checking her watch, worrying that she would not get home before Dad did. I knew that Mom would be in trouble if Dad ever found out she had been to the fairground alone.

"Okay, kids," she said anxiously, "we need to get back and start preparing dinner. Your dad will be home soon."

Raylene and I quickly returned to Mom and made our way home. We both knew the risk that Mom had taken by allowing us to visit the fair, and we didn't want Dad to find out either. I don't think that Dad ever did find out. But I continued to watch Mom live on the precipice of her emotions, never free to live her own life without fear. Therefore, we did not either. Looking back, I can recall my emotional turbulence, which was a blend of hatred, anger, grief/loss, fear, guilt, shame and confusion.

Escaping Dad

Three years later, I was trying to perfect my wheelies as I cycled up and down the tenement-lined street of Hayburn Crescent, where I lived. It was a cold and crisp January afternoon when I heard the callings of Mom echoing down the street.

"David! David!" Mom shouted from the entrance of the close—the tiled entrance corridor to the block of apartments in which we and our neighbors lived—and impatiently gestured to me to return home.

Feeling confused by my mother's impatience, I raced back toward home and shouted, "What?"

As I neared the front of the building, I saw Mom standing in the entrance of the close with a suitcase. Raylene was trailing behind her, looking upset. As I approached Mom, a taxi pulled up beside the pavement.

Mom was gentle in her approach, but she firmly took hold of my arm and bent down so that she was at eye level and said, "We're going to go and stay at Nana's for the night, David. So, get in the taxi."

Nana had shown her concern about Mom living with Dad on many occasions. I left my bike by the front step of the old building and quickly climbed into the back of the taxi with Mom and Raylene. Filled with a sense of confusion and curiosity, I stared at the suitcase and asked, "Why are we taking such a big suitcase, Mom? We've never taken a suitcase to Nana's before!"

While I waited for Mom to answer, I watched her looking anxiously out of the back window of the taxi. Tears began to well up in Mom's eyes as she begged the driver to drive us to Glasgow Central Station. That was nowhere near Nana's house.

"I only have seventy-two pence! Can you take us to Central Station?" she pleaded, desperately trying to control her tears.

The driver agreed and took us into Glasgow City Centre and dropped us off at the train station. Mom quickly walked into the main area of the station, where her Aunt Maggie from Belfast was waiting for us. After receiving a tearful call from Mom, she had agreed to help us escape to Belfast. As she sobbed in the arms of her Aunt Maggie, Mom responded to a tug at her arm. Turning around, she could see the look of confusion and fear on my face and Raylene's face.

"You said we were going to visit Nana," I said with a suspicious tone. "Why are we in the train station, Mom?"

Mom bent down and firmly grasped my and Raylene's hands in her attempt to offer some reassurance. "We're going to go and stay in Belfast for a little while, okay?" Mom had been born in Belfast and had lived there until she was thirteen.

Through her tears, Mom tried to explain as best she could, but naturally found it difficult to tell her children that she was terrified of living with their dad.

"What about Dad?" Raylene asked, looking very confused. "Will he be meeting us here, or over there?"

"No, he won't be coming with us," Mom replied. "Now come on, let's get on the train." Mom picked up her suitcase and we all began walking toward the train.

That afternoon Mom, Raylene and I and our aunt boarded the train from Glasgow Central Station and traveled to Stranraer. After a long train journey, we finally reached the harbor where we would board the ferry to Larne. I stared anxiously at the ferry that would be Mom's long-awaited escape over the Irish Sea.

As I watched Mom and awaited her next directions, a wave of nausea seemed to engulf her, because the color drained from her face. Grabbing hold of her aunt to stabilize herself, Mom began to cry. "I left him! I've really left Hamish for good this time!"

As the boat sailed toward Northern Ireland, the violent waves of the Irish Sea caused many people to be seasick. On the open deck of the ferry, I was munching my way through packets of ketchup-flavored potato chips. As I watched the violent and unpredictable waves of the Irish Sea, the gale-force winds drove the heavy rain hard against my ice-cold face.

I started to shiver as the rain began to sting my cheeks, but I did not care. I would finally be free from the brutality of my father. Finally, the ferry arrived in Larne, and Mom's Aunt Maggie quickly found a taxi that took us all into Strandtown in Belfast, where we would stay in a Loyalist area. A Loyalist area is where Protestant inhabitants maintain political views for keeping Northern Ireland within the United Kingdom, as opposed to Irish Catholic nationalists, who seek to have a unified Ireland that is separate from the United Kingdom.

After a month of living in Belfast, I finally began to settle into a routine again and started to attend Strandtown Primary School. Life was much calmer now than it had been in Glasgow, but I still had bed-wetting problems. I was much happier living in Belfast, but the thought of Dad turning up was always lurking in the back of my mind. I knew the day would eventually come when I would see Dad again. I was not exactly sure how I felt about that, because I loved Dad but also hated how he made me feel frightened.

Flying Home

One afternoon, when I returned home from school, Mom told Raylene and me that Dad was on his way over to see us all.

"Is he coming to live with us in Belfast?" I asked.

Mom sat down at the kitchen table and signaled for Raylene and me to join her.

"No, David. But your dad and I have been talking, and we're going to think about us all living together again."

"So, everything's okay between you and Dad now, then?" Raylene inquired with a hesitant tone.

"We still have a lot to talk about, but yes," Mom assured her, "I think I can say that everything is going to be okay."

That night, I lay on my bunk bed in the attic, listening to the rain as it pelted against the slate roof. I always loved listening to the sound of the rain pounding on the roof as I lay nice and warm in bed.

One night sometime later, I heard the doorbell ring and the sound of Mom's footsteps as she answered the door. I had not heard Dad's voice for months, and I was relieved that he wasn't shouting, and that Mom wasn't crying either.

When I awoke the next morning, I found Mom, Dad and Raylene sitting around the breakfast table. Dad looked up from talking with Raylene and saw me standing nervously in the kitchen doorway.

"Hello, Son." Dad pulled out a chair next to him and called me to come and sit there. With nervous anticipation, I cautiously walked over to join my family at the kitchen table, not knowing what to expect.

"Your mother and I have decided to make peace, Son," Dad said with a smile. "No more arguments. I've said I'm sorry and made peace with your mother, so everything is all right now. Okay, Son?"

I looked over at Mom as she nodded in agreement. "Does that mean we get to fly on a plane back home, Mom?"

Dad smiled at my response to the news and rubbed the top of my head playfully.

"Aye, Son!" Dad said with a chuckle. "You're not bothered that your dad's back in the picture! Aye! You just want to fly home on a plane!"

Early that afternoon, we left Belfast, as Dad took us all back to the Victorian apartment building in Hyndland, Glasgow.

Fresh Start

Dad and Mom decided that it was time for the family to have a fresh start. Once again, we moved to a different house, but this time we moved to a beautiful bungalow in a place called Bishopbriggs, just outside of Glasgow. Number 7 Eldon Gardens was far enough away from the crowded tenement streets, and the area had pleasant rosebush gardens. I distinctly remember the words my father said to me as we pulled into the driveway of our new home.

"Son, you're going to love this place! No noisy kids in the street or loud motorbikes and freight trains—just tweeting birds that'll wake ye up in the morning!"

But once again, I was the new boy in town and found myself being bullied at school. I hated school. One day, I sat in class and gazed out of the classroom window. My attention was drawn to a sea gull perched on top of a streetlamp. As I gazed upon this bird, I imagined what it would be like to spread my wings and fly away—but I quickly realized that such thoughts were nothing more than a mere flight of fancy.

It was not long before the promises of a happy and blissful life faded away and Mom and Dad began arguing again. I often questioned how anyone could ever want to be married, if this is how it really was. Dad was always the smiling and talkative personality who managed to appear as "Mr. Good Guy" and no one really saw the misery we all experienced on a daily basis. No one saw the fear. No one saw the bed-wetting. No one saw the physical slaps. No one saw the deep sense of isolation. No one saw when I cut myself with pencil sharpener blades because of the increasing rage and self-loathing I felt. I lived in a home environment where love and intimacy were twisted up with a deep sense of obligation, conformity to rules and a desperate lack of authenticity.

Seed for Thought
"We live by faith, not by sight" (Second Corinthians 5:7).

CHAPTER FOUR

David–Addiction

"Vision without action is merely a dream. Action without vision just passes the time. Vision with action can change the world." —Joel A. Barker

My parents continued their lifelong pattern of splitting up and getting back together again. Dad continued with his abusive behavior and my life continued to be full of uncertainty. It was not unusual for Raylene and me to be left in a state of shock after Dad had slapped us hard across the sides of our faces. I grew to hate my dad, and I spent as much time as possible out of the house. My nana used to tell me that when I was old enough, I could creep into my dad's room at night while he slept and could "stick a knife right through him." There were many times throughout my life, even as an adult, where I fantasized about doing the deed. But thankfully, I had a deep sense of morality and self-restraint.

After Mom and Dad got back together, we spent just under five years of living among the serenity and peacefulness of the tweeting birds and colorful rosebushes of Eldon Gardens in Bishopbriggs. I once again found myself being silently and quickly uprooted from our lovely home. The roots I had begun to form were violently ripped away again when we moved to Old Kilpatrick on the outskirts of Glasgow.

I now had to travel to Braidfield High School in Drumry, which took around fifteen minutes on the train. I consoled myself with the fact that I only had about one year left of high school. Once again being the new boy at school, I continued to have difficulty concentrating or listening due to the constant uprooting and chaos at home. However, I soon sought other ways to quiet my intense emotions—alcohol was one of them, which soon led to drugs.

Out of Control
When I attended high school in Drumry, I became friends with Jimmy. We spent a lot of time hanging around the streets after school. Jimmy was from Dalmuir, which was about a mile away from my house in Old Kilpatrick. We always hung around on the streets of Dalmuir.

"Hey, Jimmy, let's get drunk tonight," I said, smiling, while pulling four cans of Carlsberg Special Brew beer and a bottle of El Dorado tonic wine from underneath my coat.

"Did you just steal that?" Jimmy asked. I told him that I bought it.

Jimmy and I always got so drunk that we would violently vomit. As the months rolled by, it was not long before I was also regularly consuming whiskey and vodka. The era of innocence was now long gone, as I sank steadily into the murky depths of heavy alcohol abuse. After leaving school a few weeks before my sixteenth birthday, I enrolled in a basic engineering course at the Clydebank Technical College.

When I came home from college, I would quickly gulp down my dinner as fast as I could and hit the streets for some fun. Alcohol was a major part of my life by this time, and I got drunk regularly. It was not uncommon for me to be drunk every day of the week. My abuse of alcohol grew to such an extreme that I became well known to many people in the community. However, my popularity soon exposed me to other acquaintances, who introduced me to the drug culture.

Through my acquaintances, I met Scott, who in turn introduced me to some local drug dealers. I began to abuse any drug I could get my hands on. This included cannabis, amphetamine sulphate (speed), acid (LSD), ecstasy, cocaine and eventually heroin.

I soon began to realize that my life was spiraling out of control, but I still wasn't ready to give up drugs completely. My use and abuse of alcohol and illicit drugs had become so intense that sobriety left me feeling bored, angry and unfulfilled in life. Abstinence confronted me with the realities from which I sought to escape and only made me feel even worse. I had nowhere to go, nothing to do and no sense of vision or direction for the future.

Mom and Dad had another separation for a couple of months, until one day, I came home for my evening meal. My dad was sitting with a police colleague, and as I entered the room, Dad said to me, "I've asked the Lord into my life, Son, and He's going to sort out everything as He sees fit."

Dad then started going to church, and I started to see a big change in him. So, I visited Mom and told her what was going on. After a few days, she came back to collect the rest of her belongings. As she vocalized her threats to never return, Dad said, "Okay, but will you just come to church with me before you go?"

As she agreed, Mom and Dad both went to church together, and that was all I knew until I came home later that Sunday afternoon. Entering the house, I walked into the lounge and I looked at Mom and Dad, who were sitting beside each other, smiling at me. This was strange because Mom and Dad did not smile like this. I saw an amazing change in both of them, as Mom said, "I've asked Jesus to come into my life."

Weeks went by and I then went along to church with them. Shortly thereafter, I asked Jesus to come into my life and change me.

I started attending church and reading the Bible. It wasn't long before my life started to change for the good. But I felt tremendous difficulty fitting in to a church culture that was squeaky clean and where people had great difficulty relating to others who had spent most of their lives outside of the religious fishbowl.

It wasn't long before I went right off the rails and headed back down the old roads from which I had previously come. Alcohol and illicit drugs gripped my life once again for another year or two before I decided to book myself into a Christian rehabilitation center called Teen Challenge. However, while I was there, I met Kyle. He became a friend whose relationship would soon lead me back into the world of drugs. As I walked outside with Kyle through the snow in between our various classes, we spoke with a nostalgic tone and reminisced about our lives in and around the drug culture.

"This place is crap!" I muttered, as I munched on my favorite packet of ketchup chips that I had just taken from my secret bedroom stash. I had found myself beginning to crave the experiences of drug intoxication again.

"I know, man," Kyle agreed in a frustrated tone. "I miss that rush I once had from popping some E, and now all we get is constant cups of tea and 'pie-in-the-sky' sermons!"

Kyle and I laughed and mocked the Christian counselors who worked at the rehab center. Then one thing led to another, and soon I was back on the road with Kyle, traveling to England in pursuit of some excitement.

Chasing Freedom

"Freedom!" I shouted ecstatically, with my head hanging out of the small red Ford Fiesta. I spun the car around a corner and almost lost control. We knew we were going to be homeless, but neither of us cared. All we wanted were the drugs that we had craved during two long months in Teen Challenge.

I asked, "Hey, Kyle, how much money do you have?" as I tried to light a cigarette while driving the car on the bleak and winding road. It had been months since I had even been allowed a cigarette, and now I could feel my body fill with adrenaline at the thought of getting high with drugs again.

Kyle replied, "I don't even have enough money for a smoke! All I have is the clothes that I am sitting in. What about you?"

I sighed and said, "The same, man! We need to find some money fast!"

As we drove aimlessly, I began to wonder how I could possibly raise the funds for our next venture with drugs. "I have an idea," I said. "Let's turn left down here. I'm going to sell my car!"

As I pulled over, Kyle asked, "Are you sure, David? That's the only possession you have to your name!"

As I started the engine of my car, I turned toward Kyle with a serious look on my face. "Kyle, I want drugs so bad that I would sell my soul if I could right now. Let's go and sell my car!"

As we drove along, I experienced a sense of freedom to do what I wanted without any constraints being placed upon me by anyone. My life had felt empty and bland for too long, and I knew that the euphoric effects of drugs would make me feel alive again.

An hour later, my car was sold to a second hand car dealer in the Linwood area. Kyle and I were back on the streets with over 900 British pounds (over $1,200 US) in our pockets. We were given a ride to Glasgow Central Station by the second-hand car dealer and quickly bought two one-way train tickets and boarded the train. We then traveled to Wigan in Lancashire, Northern England.

Once we arrived, we went to stay with some drug dealers Kyle knew. The following morning, we hit the streets with no idea of where we were going to stay that night. Within the hour, we found a housing office where we asked if we could get any possible assistance regarding accommodations. Ten minutes later, they found accommodations for us at a local Salvation Army hostel in Saint Helens in Merseyside.

Alone with Danger

Once we had checked in at the hostel, I began to identify the main players in the local drug community. It was not long before I was fully immersed in drug use, my favorite drug being speed at that time. I always felt as if I was "king of the castle," and I did not miss anything that took place around me. I was sharp and I knew it, and I managed to stay a few steps ahead of my various acquaintances. Unfortunately, I got very indulgent with drugs and was taking ridiculous amounts of speed.

One day, I took a full half-ounce (fourteen grams). It was a Friday morning around eleven o'clock, and once again I was sitting alone, doing drugs. However, this time something felt very wrong. As I sat upright on the side of my bed, I could almost feel my heart pounding right out of my chest. With sweat pouring down my face, I began to panic.

Great! I thought. *Where are my friends now?*

Nervously, I made my way down to the reception area and asked the receptionist where the nearest hospital was located.

"Are you okay?" the receptionist asked in alarm, no doubt noticing that I looked seriously ill. "You should let me call you an ambulance."

I continued to walk out of the hostel. "I'll be okay, just leave me!" I yelled, with an irritated tone.

As I began to walk in the direction of the hospital, I did not have any idea where I was going, and I felt overwhelmed by fear. Every step I took felt as though it might be my last step. I could feel my heart racing at around four beats per second. As I got to the entrance doors of the hospital, I began to feel dizzy, and my body started to feel numb.

Maybe I truly had done what I said I would do—sell my soul for the drugs.

"Please, God," I prayed. "Please keep me alive. I promise that I'll give up drugs!"

I started to feel an overwhelming sense of loneliness and sadness. My sister, Raylene, was due to visit me from her home in southern England the very next day, and I wanted to be alive to see her. I knew that my drug abuse was dangerously out of control and my life was now in danger.

As I staggered into the emergency department at Whiston Hospital, I was quickly placed on a bed. Nurses and doctors removed my shirt and hooked me up to an ECG (electrocardiogram) monitor. A nurse then quickly tried to find a vein to insert an intravenous cannula.

I grew increasingly agitated, and the nurse who was trying to insert a needle quickly became impatient. "Sir, you need to lie down and let us help you!" she said.

As the nurse continued to fight to get a needle secured in my arm, I began to panic. Beads of sweat were pouring down my face. I knew I needed to lie still, but I had an overwhelming fear that I was going to die.

I said in my mind, "Please help me, Lord…I don't want to die!" as I tried to sit up in the bed.

The nurse snapped and said, "Sir, will you please stay still, otherwise we can't get the needle in. Without the needle, we can't give you the drugs you need!"

Judgment and Discrimination

Some of the nurses were now rolling their eyes at each other as they continued to fight to care for me. These nurses had to deal with people like me every day—druggies who never knew when to stop taking drugs. I could sense the stigma and discrimination from some of the nurses, who appeared to be exhausted from having to deal with "low-lifes" like me. They no doubt felt that after all their hard work to save my life, I, like the others they had cared for, would simply return to a drug-abusing lifestyle. I was just another druggie to them. I was someone who would reluctantly listen to their lectures about giving up drugs, only to discharge myself the next day, after a few rude comments and sarcastic good-byes.

After leaving the hospital, I frantically ran back toward the hostel, knowing that my sister was due to arrive. All I could think about was Raylene arriving at the hostel, only to be told that I was nowhere to be seen. I desperately wanted to see my big sister, and I was worried that she might have already left to return home.

As I ran into the entrance of the hostel, I was relieved to find Raylene sitting in the hostel dining room with Kyle. I was so glad to see her. She looked amazing, as always. Wearing the same clothes I'd been wearing for weeks and unshaven, I realized that I probably didn't look so good.

As I walked into the dining room, Raylene's eyes filled with tears. She told me she was astounded at how much weight I had lost. As Raylene cried, she begged me to stop taking drugs.

"I know! I'm finished for good this time!" I told her. "I promise, Ray, this is it! No more drugs!" I put my hand in my pocket, pulled out a quarter ounce of cannabis, and placed it on the table. "I'm done with it this time, Ray!" I insisted. "I've had enough of living like this!" Raylene had a successful management career and lived with her fiancée in a lovely rural village in the County of Kent—which was known as the Garden of England because of its many orchards and beautiful countryside.

Shame

After much discussion about drugs and the drug culture, Raylene took me out and bought me a new pair of shoes. All that I owned was a psychedelic shirt, the beads that hung around my neck, and the pair of jeans and boots that I wore day in and day out. Like the many homeless people I knew, I had no underwear, greasy facial hair and smelly feet.

As I walked through the shopping center with Raylene, I began to feel vulnerable, as if the whole world was staring at me. I knew that I looked terrible, but as people continued to stare at me, I felt a sense of hate, vulnerability, dependence and shame. I felt angry at their judgmental eyes, resentful at their perceived affluent status, and shamed by my own inabilities to fit in a "normal" society where I could "contribute."

I knew that I owed Raylene so much, but I had nothing to offer her in return. I had to simply receive her help with no strings attached, and this was hard for me to accept. I contemplated ending my drug abuse but was so ambivalent at the same time. After getting some shoes and some money, I walked Raylene to the train station, where I watched her board a train back to her home in southern England. As I sat alone on the bench at the station, I watched as Raylene's train became smaller and smaller as it meandered its way down the tracks into the distance, back toward the English countryside. As the little red light on the back of the train disappeared into the distance, I turned and looked across the railway tracks and stared at the hostel, in all its ugliness.

As I walked back to the hostel, I was filled with a perplexing combination of emotions. I thought about Jim Morrison's lyrics in the song "Break on Through (to the Other Side)" and how I could easily relate to those words. I felt as though I was standing behind some great divide in life. I could clearly see the other side, where people were alive, secure, married and content. I was able to witness this reality but was somehow unable to "break on through" into any sense of normality.

I was aware of the reality of my circumstances, yet I was also aware of the possibilities of another way of life, and I wanted it. However, I did not know how to get to it, where to go or what I needed to do. I had discovered that being homeless made me "not eligible" for so many things. Applying for jobs was difficult, as I lived in a hostel, and people would likely discriminate against me. I was not able to acquire better housing, as I was on a very long waiting list. I was not able to associate with more stable individuals since my instability, personal insecurities and physical appearance revealed who I really was and excluded me. I was the so-called lowlife who had no fixed abode.

Yet I also quickly recollected the true nature of genuine friendship and knew that I wasn't as alone as I may have thought. There were people I knew in Glasgow who would be supportive of me. I had some decent contacts. I had Mom and Dad, and I had a local church where I once had some contact. I had fully experienced the uncomfortable discrimination that accompanied homelessness. The stigma I had once never believed existed had now become my reality.

But like my father before me, I simply hopped right back on that merry-go-round of denial and abuse.

Overdosing and Intravenous Drugs

I slowly overcame the trauma of my previous overdose, and the promises of giving up drugs had once again faded from my memory. Instead of quitting, I started to use intravenous methadone ampuls and heroin. My painful state of being was too much to bear, and I told myself that "I need to relax."

I was tired of constantly feeling the paranoid effects of amphetamines, which made me think that I needed to keep looking over my shoulder. Opiates helped me solve this problem. I found that I still had my "sharpness," but I was more relaxed at the same time. This allowed me to convey a more confident and controlled disposition within the various subcultures in which I had acquaintances.

I got my first "intravenous fix" from a guy called Bill, who agreed to inject me. I had always smoked heroin or popped pills, but now I found myself agreeing to inject heroin directly into my veins.

"I feel guilty about doing this," said Bill as he was searching for a vein, "but if you really want it, then here goes."

I felt the sharp puncturing of my skin as Bill inserted the needle into my vein and injected me with heroin. That was it. I was immediately baptized into the culture of intravenous drug use. Heroin felt nice.

One overdose led to another, and eventually I found myself sitting on the edge of my bed in the Salvation Army hostel. I was scared. I had injected too much intravenous methadone (a pharmaceutically prescribed heroin substitute) and couldn't feel my own pulse. My breathing was extremely shallow. I also felt a measure of motor impairment that resembled the onset of paralysis. I could feel myself going into respiratory arrest.

As I lay there alone, I felt that my vital organs wanted to shut down, and I could feel my limbs becoming weak. Incense sticks were deliberately jammed into small holes that I had made in my walls. I had done this so that I could lie on my bed and watch their suspended tips glow in the darkness of my room. Their glowing tips burned brightly, emitting a rich sandalwood fragrance and reminding me of the small red light on the back of Raylene's train. In the smoky atmosphere, I frantically rummaged through the remaining cubes of cannabis resin, pharmaceutical pills and methadone bottles in my top drawer and pulled out a photograph of Raylene.

Life or Death
As I stared at the picture of my sister, I recalled the era of innocence in the early seventies and how I used to laugh. My whole life quickly flashed before my eyes—how I used to be excited about Santa Claus at Christmastime, how I used to listen to the Eagles and T. Rex on the radio and how I used to be an innocent kid at school with all the same choices in life as my colleagues had.

Then there was the bed-wetting, the family separations and the black hole that enveloped my existence. *How did I get here?* I wondered. *When did life become so complicated?*

I struggled to stop myself from collapsing onto the vomit-stained floor as my situation became more intense. *This was not meant to happen. I am David. I am the son of a policeman! Brought up in a good…well, okay, family. This only happens to the stereotypical junkie, not to me!*

As I sat on the edge of my bed that night, I battled with life and death decisions. I thought about Raylene and my parents' smiles. I rummaged around my drawers looking for pictures of my sister. My life had previously meant very little. Yet now, I suddenly had a deeper appreciation of life in all of its fullness as I was confronted with a reality that I had never even contemplated before.

I had finally come to my senses after years of substance abuse and felt an unusually fresh sense of hope for the future. The metaphorical light had been switched on. I lay down on my bed, trying to control my breathing. With the incense sticks glowing in the silent darkness, I began to consider a clear plan of action that involved complete abstinence from all harmful substances. I was terrified that I would never wake up but eventually drifted off to sleep.

The next morning, I scrambled together a small amount of change so I could buy a half bottle of wine called MD20-20, otherwise known as "Mad Dog." I quickly guzzled the alcoholic "goodness" in order to calm my early withdrawal symptoms. *At least I am not doing drugs,* I thought.

New Beginnings

Later in the morning, as I sat with my acquaintance Mickie in the hostel, I told him that I was finished with drug abuse. Mickie was shocked. I could see the sense of alarm on his face as he became aware of the finality of our relationship and his ever-increasing loneliness.

"Don't be stupid!" he said. "You just had a bad hit, man, that's all! Next time will be great again!" Mickie continued to try to convince me. He even offered me free intravenous drugs and asked me to consider the possible error of my ways.

"Mickie, I'm done, man!" I insisted. "I'm tired and I don't want to live like this anymore!" I knelt on the floor and said, "Mickie, I need to clean myself up, so will you cut off my beard?" as I handed him a pair of scissors.

Mickie began to cut off my beard as an audience of drug addicts began to accumulate outside my door.

Within five minutes, I was cleanly shaven. I quickly stood up, grabbed my few belongings, and stuffed them into a bag as Mickie and a bunch of other drug addicts stood watching me.

"See you later, Mickie. I have a train to catch, and I need to get out of here!" I quickly left the hostel and went to the Saint Helen's train station to travel back home to Glasgow. I looked southbound down the tracks, where Raylene had once meandered her way into the distance, back to the Garden of England. I then looked northbound up the tracks in the opposite direction I was about to travel, back to Scotland. Hope had gripped my being, even though I had absolutely no idea how things would work out.

Once the train arrived at the platform, I quickly boarded and sat down across the aisle from a young woman and her child. Within seconds, she was staring at me with disgust and fear.

Like a model citizen with my physician-prescribed oral methadone linctus in my pocket, I quickly gulped the last mouthfuls in preparation for the journey back to Glasgow Central Station and braced myself for the forthcoming withdrawal. I could feel the judgment of everyone on the train around me in the tangible silence that reverberated around the train carriage. Other passengers could see that I was a drug user, yet none of them realized that I was no threat to them. After all, I simply wanted to join the ranks of the respectable.

I stayed in Glasgow, back at my parents' home, for a couple of months. During this time, after much deliberation, I decided to get involved with the Christian rehabilitation service with which I was previously involved. However, as I wanted to escape from all the familiar faces and places in Scotland, I was fortunate enough to be allocated a place in an induction rehab center in Wigan, Northern England. After five months in Wigan, I traveled to the main national rehabilitation center in Penygroes in South Wales. I undertook the rehabilitation program for almost a year before becoming a member of the staff.

Twelve months later, I decided to apply to undertake a degree in theology at Regents Theological College. This private theological college was affiliated with Manchester University. As I completed my application, I wondered whether I would even be capable of completing a degree course. However, I was accepted into the program and was soon immersed in my studies.

I was a reformed drug addict, and almost none of my fellow students had even heard of some of the things that I had experienced in my own life. I felt very out of place, and it was quite difficult to adapt. Yet I eventually managed to overcome obstacles I had once considered insurmountable, such as adhering to academic deadlines, living a life that was drug-free, and actually having attainable goals and aspirations for the future.

I enjoyed having a quiet life for once, one that was not full of complications and chaos. I often sat alone in the library, studying for hours, before walking back to my room to sit alone again. I found it difficult to relate to the other students, many of whom were from wealthy Christian families. I knew that some of them did not understand me, and I noticed them staring.

One evening, as I was getting my team together to do our assigned "wash-up" duty, I noticed that one of the students was missing.

"Does anyone know where Rachel is?" I asked. "She didn't turn up yesterday either."

"She and her roommate are usually out together acting up to no good," a young guy yelled as he continued to load the noisy dishwasher.

What is it with these entitled people? I thought.

All they were asked to do was to wash a few dishes, and even that was too much for some of the "princesses" (a generic and derogatory term used to describe a spoiled and overindulged individual, irrespective of their specific gender) I now found myself having to deal with. I threw down my tea towel and walked over toward the Bolton block of mixed-gender halls of residence, which was separated from the foreign language school halls of residence. I was determined to make an impression.

These kids have no idea what rough is, I thought as I walked toward Bolton block. I found myself feeling irritated by the ability of the wealthy students to seemingly get through life without any complications at all. Well, it was time that someone gave these "princesses" a large dose of reality.

It was not until we had been married for many years that I told Rachel how I had felt like an idiot when I walked away after the heated argument in Bolton block over her nonappearance in the kitchen where she was supposed to be on the dishwashing rotation. *But how could I have known that she was sick?* I asked myself after she had slammed the door in my face.

I had found myself judging in exactly the same way that I had once been judged by society. As I left Bolton block and walked back toward the kitchen, I began to feel a little guilty about how I had treated Rachel, who was simply not feeling well. I decided that my first priority would be to make amends with her the following day.

She was kind of cute, I thought, smiling to myself. *And no girl has ever dared to slam the door in my face before.*

The next day, I walked into communication class and saw that Rachel was sitting alone, deep in thought. As I watched her, I began to wonder if perhaps she was different from other girls I had met in the college.

I soon learned that she was certainly no "princess." After getting to know Rachel a little better, I began to realize that she was the soul mate I had never thought I would find. It was years later that I shared with Rachel how I had been waiting to connect with someone like her all my life.

And with each passing day, I knew I was falling in love. And so was Rachel.

Seed for Thought
"Now to him who is able to do immeasurably more than all we ask or imagine, according to his power that is at work within us" (Ephesians 3:20).

SECTION TWO

Shoots and Leaves: Marriage

CHAPTER FIVE

Pain in Spain

*"A secret is a kind of promise…
It can also be a prison." —Jennifer Lee Carrell*

After leaving David's sister's house, we boarded the bus that would take us to our honeymoon venue. I was praying daily that everything would be resolved when we got to Spain. Maybe time alone away from all the stresses and people that we knew was what we needed to be able to relax and have sex. Spain felt a very long way on the bus, and by the time David and I had reached France, my legs had started to cramp up, and I was feeling a little sick and dehydrated. The tour guide was desperately trying to keep her tour group calm. Standing at the hotel desk, she attempted to shout as loud as she could over the crowded hotel lobby.

"Everybody! Please listen! The bedrooms will not be ready for another few hours yet, so please be patient with us," the tour guide squawked as she tried to keep all of her very tired group calm. "If anyone feels like exploring, there are some tasty restaurants and some great shops that you can experience while you wait. Just make sure you are back around 5:00 p.m. Your rooms should be ready then."

The tour guide nervously smiled at her very annoyed and tired-looking tour group, as she quickly made her escape.

Time

I felt an immense sense of relief that I had been given a little more time to spend with David before we had to reenter the nightmare—the bedroom—that we had blissfully forgotten about for a couple of days. Although, this time we were officially on our honeymoon, so I felt even more pressure to resolve my humiliating issue. The last few days we had stayed overnight with family members, so trying to resolve our bedroom issues was not at the top of the agenda. We didn't want to share with family about our struggles, so we put on our fake smiles while we visited with family. Walking through Pineda de Mar, I glanced around at the streets that now oozed with sexuality. Women with perfect bodies walked around in their revealing dresses and swimsuits, hand in hand with their partners, who looked just as good. They all looked so happy and relaxed, while I stood feeling unsexual, wearing a pair of white shorts with a green T-shirt, trainers and no suntan.

Honeymoon Fears

Later, after we finished a big meal at the hotel, a waiter came over to our table with a little cake that had sparklers on it. The whole tour group then began to clap and cheer as David and I watched our sparklers fizzle out. The tour group had somehow found out that we had just gotten married. As I watched the sparklers on the cake fizzle out, with the sound of the tour group clapping and cheering in the distance, panic unexpectedly gripped me. *What if my marriage fizzles out as quickly as those sparklers did?*

Suddenly my thoughts were interrupted by an older-looking woman wearing a suit. After vacantly studying her, I realized that she was our tour guide.

"David, I hope you and Rachel will be joining us this evening for some singing and a short Bible talk. We will be starting in around thirty minutes."

David shot a quick glance toward me before turning back to the tour guide. "Oh, thank you, but Rachel and I are quite exhausted after the long journey. I think we will pass tonight, if you don't mind." I sensed that David felt a little guilty for not joining in the group activities the tour guide had prepared for us.

"Yeah, I'm exhausted after that long journey—all I want to do is sleep!" I agreed, yawning for effect.

"That's fine, as long as we see you at some of the meetings this week," she replied in a serious tone.

As the tour lady strolled back to her group, I knew she was probably now wondering why a newlywed couple would book themselves on a group tour if they didn't want to join in group activities. After returning to our hotel room, I still found myself worrying about what the tour guide thought of us.

"I bet she thinks we are snobs now," I whispered as I lay on the bed next to David. Wrapped in David's arms, I continued, "If only she knew what we were going through, David. I am sure that if she knew about our issue, she wouldn't be so bemused with our lack of participation in their rooftop sing-along. If only she knew."

David grew annoyed with my constant worries about not pleasing those around us. "Well, I don't feel guilty, Rachel. We don't have to attend any meetings if we don't want to. This is our getaway, and this is our honeymoon, not theirs."

"I just wish we had been able to afford that honeymoon in Greece. There would have been no stupid tour guides there trying to push us into church meetings," I said as I jumped off the bed to head into the shower.

Hitting a Brick Wall

After days of nervous anticipation, David and I had finally found ourselves alone again, and we both knew that this was the perfect time for us to attempt intercourse again. Awkwardly, we began to kiss, and soon we both felt our excitement heighten, touching each other's bodies sensually. Caressing each other with intensity, our breathing became faster. I could feel myself longing for David. As David kissed my body, I could feel him slowly starting to push against the entrance to my vagina. A surge of excitement shot through my body, causing me to gasp for breath. Then suddenly, as David began to enter me, I felt every muscle in my thighs and pelvis tighten. My buttocks lifted off the bed, and suddenly, I found myself frantically pushing David away.

"Stop! Please! Stop! It's not working, David! Please, it hurts so much!" I yelled. For a second, it felt like everything in time had frozen as David sat on the bed stunned, and I wept uncontrollably.

I quickly got off the bed and walked over to the bathroom. I could see the concern on David's face and the sheer shock that it had happened again. With a confused and frustrated tone in his voice, he asked, "I don't understand why this is happening. What is wrong with you?"

Standing anxiously in the doorway of the bathroom, I desperately tried to choke back my tears of humiliation so that I could reply. "I don't know, David, I really don't, but it's impossible! I can't even begin to describe how painful it is, and that's only at the entrance. I can't see how it is ever going be possible to get you inside of me!"

Some might question if the pain I was experiencing was the pain of losing my virginity, but it did not matter how many times we tried, the pain did not disappear, and it seemed like I could not get past a few inches without experiencing excruciating pain.

David and I tried so many times to have sex on our honeymoon, but each attempt ended in failure. Unable to consummate our marriage, we were left feeling even more frustrated, upset and confused. Every time David attempted to have intercourse with me, I responded in exactly the same manner.

"You need to stop tensing your legs, Rachel. You're tensing so much that I can barely even see a hole!" David exclaimed with frustration in his voice. I would cry with pain again and again, begging him to stop.

"I'm sorry, okay! I don't seem to be able to stop myself from tensing! It feels like I am too small and every time you try, it feels like there are knives searing through my vagina!"

It seemed as if it was impossible for David to get more than a third of the way in, without me experiencing intolerable pain. Every day we tried different sexual positions, and we even tried showering together to make it more romantic. Yet it seemed that no matter how many times we tried and no matter which way we tried, we still hit what was beginning to feel like a brick wall.

Every time we attempted sexual intercourse, David would physically watch the muscles in my thighs violently tense. It was useless, and trying to get uninterrupted time alone was also a problem. The leader of the tour group had continued to vocalize her expectations that everyone attend her scheduled Bible meetings.

One morning, David and I decided to attempt the impossible again. "Okay, just relax, Rachel; it's going to work this time," David said, while he continued to kiss me. "You just need to relax your thighs." I desperately tried to concentrate on stopping the usual narration that had now began to occur in my mind whenever we tried to have sex.

"Room service!" the maid shouted impatiently as she loudly knocked on our hotel room door. Without any notice, the bedroom door flung wide open and in walked an old Spanish woman of small stature. Quickly, I fled from the bed and ran into the bathroom. David remained in bed while the maid stood frozen and shocked, looking embarrassed and flustered.

"I am so sorry, sir," she said as she quickly left the room. Knowing that someone could walk into our room at any time really did not help the situation we had found ourselves in. As I cautiously crept back toward the bed, David knew that our situation was not getting any better, and he knew he had to address this matter head on.

Walls of Silence
"We really need to talk to someone, Rachel. Why don't you phone Ruth, Rebekah or your mom?" Ruth was a close friend from college, and Rebekah was a friend I had had since childhood and we remain friends today. "Talking to another woman might help you!"

I knew that David was right, but how could I ever confide in someone about such a humiliating problem? Even though they were lifelong friends, I could not bring myself to share something so shameful and humiliating. What would they say? How could they ever understand an issue like this? Even if I did share this with them, it's not like they would know what to do or even what to say.

"I can't, David! It's too embarrassing! I already feel like a freak! Please! We can never tell anybody about this! Please, promise me that you won't tell anybody! I can't bear the thought of anyone knowing what a freak I am." The shame I felt was deep-rooted; I should be able to have sex like everybody else. The thought of the disappointment my family would feel, that I had failed at the very beginning of my marriage, made me want to just deny that anything was wrong.

As I sat on the edge of the bed, once again my eyes filled with tears. I had begun to feel like I had cried for most of my honeymoon. The intense feelings of loss and hopelessness were becoming familiar, and I seemed to wake up to them every morning. Interrupting my never-ending deep thoughts, David continued to insist that I talk with somebody.

"Phone your mom then…speaking to her might help!" Annoyed and frustrated by my lack of response, he continued, "I don't know what else to suggest, Rachel! We are so alone with this problem and we need help! Maybe I should speak with my parents, then?"

Turning my face sharply toward David, I yelled, "No! Please, David! I am begging you! Please don't tell them! They will tell you to leave me, and they will think I am a freak!"

Deflated and exhausted from looking for solutions, David stood up and walked over to the door. "Well! I don't know what to suggest then, Rachel! We need a solution to this problem! I can't live like this; in fact, I don't want to live like this! So, we need to find a solution and fast." Slamming the door behind him, David was gone.

As I lay on the hotel bed, I began to feel the intensity and the seriousness of my issue, and I felt full of shame. The last thing I wanted was for David's family to find out that their only son had married a "freak of nature"! David had only gone for a walk this time; however, I knew that it would only be a matter of time before he would keep on walking and never come back.

I often created and listened to my self-limiting stories. Thoughts raced through my head, and I believed them. *You will never overcome this. You are such a freak of nature. David would be better off without you. You are so selfish, making him stay in this relationship. A real woman would leave and just let him go. It would be better for him if you just died; then he could be* happy. *You will always be this way. There is something physically wrong with you that can never be fixed. It is always going to be this way, so you should just give in.*

I constantly listened to stories like this in my mind, day in and day out. I did not realize that these stories were preventing me from moving forward or finding a solution. Every time I thought of sex, I was flooded with negative thoughts of how it would be. I could no longer see any positive aspects; all I seemed to focus on was what could go wrong. Even when I was trying to have sex, the thoughts would flood my head.

I knew that David was right—I did need to talk with someone. But who? The only person I could phone was my mom. How could I tell her about my shameful disorder? I knew I had no choice; I needed someone to confide in. Maybe she would be able to tell me where I should go for some help?

It's All Gone Wrong
After David returned from his walk, we walked down to the Spanish pier and found a phone booth. As the phone started to ring on the other end, I began to feel a mixture of nausea and adrenaline as I desperately tried to find the words to explain to my mom that I was struggling to have sex. The ringing stopped and there, on the other end of the phone, was my mother's voice.

"Hello," Mom said.

Hearing my mother's voice suddenly caused my eyes to well up with tears again. After gulping back the tears, I replied, "Hi, Mom, how are you doing?"

"Rachel! I didn't expect to hear from you so soon! Oh, it's wonderful to hear from you! How's the honeymoon going? Are you and David enjoying Spain?" she asked.

It seemed like the pause in my response was endless as I tried to pull myself together in order to speak. I knew that they would be upset and devastated at hearing the news that their daughter's marriage had gone dreadfully wrong after only a few days.

I could already hear the worry in my mother's voice when she asked, "Rachel, are you okay? Why are you crying? Is everything okay with you and David?"

"It's all gone wrong! I don't even know how to begin to tell you what's happened," I replied in floods of tears. I continued to explain how I had experienced intolerable pain whenever I had attempted to engage in sex. Although I felt humiliated and ashamed at sharing this embarrassing information with my mom, I immediately felt some relief that I had managed to confide in someone.

"You will need to make an appointment with the doctor when you get home. You might need to be stretched! I had to be stretched when I was younger. It's a simple procedure and nothing to worry about," Mom said reassuringly.

"What do you mean, stretched?" I asked with a frantic and confused tone.

"Look, just try to enjoy the rest of your time away and then when you get home, you can go and see the doctor for some advice," Mom reassured.

As I hung up the phone, I stepped outside of the phone booth and strolled over to David, who patiently sat waiting on a nearby wall.

"Well? What did your mom say?" he asked.

"She said that I will need to see a doctor when I get home, because I might need to be stretched!" I replied, still looking confused at the thought of being stretched. As we walked along the pier, David proudly swung his arm around me and gave me a reassuring hug.

"Your mom's right. We will book an appointment with the doctor when we get home, and this horrible mess will get sorted. The doctor will know what to do."

In my complete lack of optimism, I moaned, "But Mom said that I might need to be stretched! Maybe I am too small down there, David! Maybe I am too small! David, this might not just be in my head!"

David let out a big sigh and replied, "Rachel, stop worrying! Whatever it is that's causing the problem, the doctors will fix it. I'm sure that they have seen this problem many times before. I know you think that you're the only woman in the world who has this problem, but I'm sure you're not. The doctor will figure it out."

Overeating and Panic

The rest of the honeymoon was spent eating and drinking at the Buccaneer Pub. Comfort food seemed to be the vice that both David and I found ourselves running to whenever we felt disillusioned.

One evening, after returning to our hotel room after an enjoyable night out, I started to feel really a strange sensation that I had never experienced before. Suddenly gasping for air, I screamed out, "I can't breathe! My heart feels like it's going to explode! What's wrong with me?"

As I sat on the hotel bed, I began to feel extremely faint and like I wasn't breathing enough. My hands suddenly began to shake, and I could feel pins and needles moving up both of my arms. As I began to pace up and down the room with sheer panic, I anxiously shrieked, "What's happening to me?"

Neither David nor I realized that I had just experienced my first panic attack, which, sadly, would be one of many I would experience over the next few years. When someone experiences a panic attack, they feel a sudden sense of impending doom and they are unable to control the physical symptoms that occur. A fast heart rate, shortness of breath, sweating, shaking and dizziness are all symptoms.

Panic attacks are an extreme form of anxiety and are often caused by environmental stimuli that may trigger flashbacks or thoughts of stressful situations, or they may be caused by unconscious thoughts that a person is not even aware of.

My panic attacks seemed to be connected to my sexual disorder. I carried extreme guilt and shame that led to thoughts that because I was not able to have sex, I would be punished by God. I was convinced that God would cause me to die so David could be free, especially since David had escaped so many other issues in his life. As the panic attack began to subside, I found myself feeling exhausted.

Climbing into bed, I started to wonder about how my life had become so out of control. It seemed like I had been in control of my life until I got married. Now it felt like my whole life had suddenly fallen to pieces.

As I turned over in bed and looked at David as he slept, I once again felt the feelings of being alone and isolated. Deep down, I knew that the future looked bleak for me and David, and I began to feel frightened at the thought of what the future might bring. Thoughts of David leaving me continued to haunt me. The tremendous sense of guilt I had started to feel for putting David through this horrible situation began to weigh heavily on me.

I loved David so much, and I longed to show him that I loved him. However, all David had felt from me was rejection. He had started to interpret my aversion to sex and the constant pleas for him to stop as a sign that I didn't truly love him.

A Slippery Slope

Although David had become more angry and bitter, he had held it together and thankfully, he had not relapsed back into drug addiction with the stress. However, up until our wedding night, David had chosen not to drink alcohol at all since he had recovered from his drug addiction.

One evening while out at the Buccaneer Pub, without warning, David walked up to the bar lady and asked for a beer. When he returned to the table, I worriedly asked, "I thought you had given up drinking?"

Staring through me, he gulped down a few mouthfuls of his beer and then turned away to look toward the people dancing on the dance floor.

"I'm okay with one or two, Rachel. I know my limits. Anyway, for just one night, I need to switch off from this horrible mess. I just want to have one night where I don't have to feel stressed!"

He did not limit himself to one or two. That night was the first time I had seen my husband drunk.

As I dragged David back to the hotel through the crowded streets of partying people, I began to feel the familiar engulfing sense of guilt. *This is all my fault! If I didn't have this stupid problem, then David wouldn't have gotten drunk!* I thought, as I threw David onto the bed and pulled off his shoes.

The next morning, I awoke to David sitting on the side of the bed, waiting for me to wake up.

"I'm so sorry, Rachel. I didn't mean to get drunk. I just felt so overwhelmed by everything." I could see by his facial expression that he felt annoyed with himself for allowing himself to get drunk. I knew that everything in him did not want to fall back into the trap of addictions again. As always, David had brought me a cup of tea, as he knew that I struggled to wake up in the morning.

As I sat up in bed, I replied with a guilty tone, "No, I'm sorry, David. This is all my fault! You would never have drunk if I hadn't inflicted you with this hellish nightmare. You should never have married me, David!"

"Rachel, that's not true! I made the decision to drink, not you. Look, I promise, it won't happen again. Okay?" David insisted.

"Okay" I replied with a flat tone. It didn't matter how many times David told me that it wasn't my fault. In my mind, this whole situation remained my fault.

I knew that David was struggling to keep my shameful secret, and I knew that it would only be a matter of time before he would have to confide in someone. I dreaded that day when David would share my shameful secret with someone else. It might be soon, as we were to visit with his parents in Málaga on our way back to England.

As I continued to pack the bags in the hotel room in Pineda de Mar, I started to run through scenarios in my head of what they would say and what they would think. David continued to offer reassurance that everything would turn out fine. I am sure that some days he felt like all he ever did was counsel and console his wife. In his frustration, David confided that those days of counseling and consoling made him feel more like he was my counselor or my father, rather than my husband.

Some days, it seemed to David like I constantly cried and even though he tried everything to console me, he sometimes found himself exhausted and defeated from trying.

David shared with me that he had never thought he would ever walk out on his wife, as I cried inconsolably. Yet at times, he found that he just had to escape. David could see the vortex of confusion and loss that I had become trapped in, and he had begun to feel powerless in helping me. He also knew that I worried about him confiding in someone. But then what was he supposed to do? He knew that this situation was too much for him to deal with alone.

He knew that he needed someone to counsel him and to understand the situation he found himself trapped in. But there was no one he could talk to and if he even suggested confiding in someone, I pleaded with him in desperation to remain quiet.

Masks of Happiness

As we walked into Hamish and Dorothy's house, I remembered the first time we had visited David's parents shortly after we had gotten engaged. Back then, David and I had been happy and neither of us had a single care in the world. Now, everything seemed tainted with the horrible realization that a serious and shameful problem stalked our every move.

Even holding hands and kissing became an effort and a constant reminder of what we had begun to desperately avoid. What had once been an enjoyable experience for David and me now only left us both with a sense of hopelessness. I knew that David now struggled to relax when he kissed me. Every time was the same because our times of sexual intimacy ended abruptly, leaving David with a constant intense feeling of rejection. Both wearing our masks of wedding bliss, we hugged and greeted David's parents.

Hamish beamed with joy at having his son visit him and Dorothy in Spain.

"It's good to see you, Son, and your lovely bride!" he said while he cheekily chuckled to himself.

With tears in her eyes, Dorothy hugged her son, and after wiping her eyes and composing herself, she said, "Oh, it's good to see you again, flunk! I've missed you!" David's parents often used this nickname for David, which is another term for failure.

While Dorothy hugged her son, Hamish turned toward me and gave me a hug. "Hello, darling, it's good to see you kids so happy."

Many things had changed in David's relationship with his parents. After he had overcome his drug addictions, he and Hamish had slowly worked at rebuilding their relationship. David could see that his parents were happy and that they had finally settled. It was clear that Dorothy had desperately missed David and Raylene since they had both moved away from home.

Once David and I had settled in, Hamish and Dorothy decided to take us for a walk around Málaga. After finding a restaurant, we all sat eating chicken while Hamish and Dorothy quizzed us about our honeymoon and talked about the wedding. Continuing to wear our fake masks of happiness, David and I continued with our efforts to convince them of our fake happiness. Yet I could tell by Hamish's facial expressions that he could sense that something didn't add up. Even though he had retired from the police force, he had never lost the art of being a cop.

As each day passed, Hamish noticed how irritable and on edge David had become. David had always found getting along with his parents difficult when they all lived under one roof, but with each day, it was becoming increasingly difficult for both of us to keep up our act of a happy couple.

One evening, David and I stood on the rooftop of Dorothy and Hamish's villa enjoying the picturesque view of the lush green mountains and the sound of the crickets. Spain should have been a dream vacation for us; instead, it turned out to be the beginning of years of torture.

Staring out into the endless distance of the mountains, David said, "Mom and Dad know something's wrong, Rachel, I can tell."

"Please don't tell me that you told them!" I anxiously whispered.

"No, I didn't say anything, but how long do I cope with something like this alone, Rachel? I have no one to confide in, and it's not fair—it's just too much to cope with alone!"

"It's the same for me! At least you can walk away from it all, David. You can walk away from me. I'm stuck with this issue. I can't walk away from it," I tearfully replied.

"Rachel, you know that walking out isn't an option for me. I love you and I made a commitment to you. I'm not going anywhere!" A part of me felt relieved that he would not walk out on me, but the other part of me felt the overwhelming pressure to find a way to resolve my issues even though I did not know where to start. I carried the guilt of feeling I had trapped my husband, a husband who had already escaped so much heartache, and now I was unintentionally causing him more pain. I was determined to resolve my issues, but I still battled the self-limiting stories I told myself daily that this would never happen—stories like, "you are never going to get over this condition," "you are such a freak of nature," and "it's only a matter of time until David walks away from you."

The complete silence of the mountains almost became deafening, as we both stared out over the rooftop veranda. Sometimes neither of us knew what to say next. It didn't matter what either of us said, as it never made us feel any better.

After a few minutes of listening to only the sound of the crickets, David said, "I think we need to leave this place early, Rachel, and get home so that we can sort this problem out."

"I agree, but what do we tell your mom and dad? They have not seen you for so long and I think they will be upset if you leave early."

"Leave it to me, Rachel. I'll sort it out, I promise."

We desperately wanted answers and an end to our hellish nightmare. As we boarded the flight back to England, little did David and I know that our nightmare was only just beginning.

Seed for Thought
"Therefore confess your sins to each other and pray for each other so that you may be healed. The prayer of a righteous man is powerful and effective" (James 5:16).

CHAPTER SIX

My Vagina Has What?

"Please don't ever think that you can't ever get out of the rut you may be in or think you can't take your life to a whole new level. Anything is possible when you have a path, a plan, and a desire to take action." —Dean Graziosi

A few weeks after returning home, I awaited yet another doctor's appointment and tried to figure out some things on my own. *Women on TV make it look so easy!* I slammed the laptop shut in frustration. I had thought that maybe watching someone else have sex would help me figure out why I struggled to have sex.

Some women can look back on their journey with vaginismus and easily identify when they first discovered that there was a problem. Personally, prior to first attempting sexual intercourse, there did not seem to be any identifiable situation where I initially realized there were any issues. Looking back many years later, I now realize that the roots had been planted very early in my childhood, and the initial pain and being unprepared for my wedding night was what I now believe led to my vaginismus.

"How stupid am I to think that there is a simple solution to my situation," I muttered, as I headed to the door and put on my jacket. As I grabbed my bag and closed the apartment door, I wondered if maybe there might be something seriously wrong with me. Maybe I had a tumor growing down there, or maybe I was too small like my mom had suggested!

As I walked through the town, I looked enviously at the young single teenage moms with strollers and the perfect couples with families lining up at the ice-cream van waiting to treat their children to ice cream. The newspapers had even reported on thirteen-year-old children who had managed to get pregnant.

Exposed
What is wrong with me? I thought.

It seemed that everyone else had it figured out, and no one else seemed to require an instruction booklet or someone to tell them what to do. Even if I had been given the luxury of an instruction booklet, it still would have failed to solve the intolerable pain I experienced every time I had sex. Surely sex is meant to be pleasurable and enjoyable. Movie stars always had smiles on their faces afterward. They did not cry during sex or experience the dread of constantly trying again and again to have sex. I could not ever recall seeing movie stars portraying themselves as living with a sexual disorder. In our neat little world, no one has such disorders; they don't exist, or so people think. As I continued to walk toward the doctor's office, it suddenly occurred to me: sex would never work for me, because for some reason, I was broken.

I put on a fake brave face as I walked into the doctor's office and checked myself in with the receptionist. Everything in me did not want to visit with my doctor, but I desperately wanted the painful knots in my stomach to go away. Since returning from Spain, visiting doctors for help with my sexual pain had not been a pleasant experience, and no one had been able to give me guidance or understanding. The overhead speaker called out my name, so I slowly stood up and walked into the doctor's office.

I sheepishly sat down in the chair and began to study the heavyset lady with short hair and round glasses as she finished writing some notes. The doctor looked up from her notes and smiled. After turning her seat toward my direction, she asked, "So, what can I do for you today, Rachel?"

"My stomach has been feeling like it has been all knotted and painful for the last week, and I've been constipated and nauseated. I just don't seem to be able to shift this feeling in my stomach." She turned back to her notes and started to write, while waving her arm toward the examination bed in the corner of her room.

"Okay, take a seat on the table, Rachel. Just pop the gown on and take off your jeans and let me know when you are ready," she instructed as she continued to write in my patient notes. After putting on the gown and positioning myself on the table, I quietly called out, "Okay! I'm ready."

"Right, Rachel, I will just examine your abdomen." As the doctor began to examine my stomach, I suddenly noticed that she was now staring down at my legs.

Oh, my goodness! I had forgotten to shave my legs! *What must she think of me?* I thought with a deep sense of embarrassment. Since I had returned from Spain, I had been so depressed and wrapped up in constant thoughts about not being able to have sex, that I had forgotten to shave my legs for the doctor's appointment. The last thing on my mind these days had been to shave my legs.

Since having this issue, I had not felt like a woman anymore. I felt like a freak, and clearly not much had been happening in the bedroom department. It had seemed pointless for me to make myself look sexy anymore. What would be the point? I already felt a deep sense of guilt, without making David desire me even more, only for me to constantly let him down at the most crucial point.

The doctor was continuing to assess my stomach, and with a puzzled look, she asked, "Do you have a partner, Rachel?"

"Yes, I just got back from my honeymoon in Spain." Without replying, the doctor finished her physical examination and turned around and walked back to her desk.

"You can put your clothes back on now," she instructed. As I jumped up to get dressed, I started to wonder why my doctor would ask such a question. Maybe my hairy legs had been a giveaway that I had issues in the bedroom?

As I nervously sat back down on the chair, I inwardly talked positively to myself to stay in control. The doctor remained silent and allowed me to talk incessantly about the wedding, as I shared the lies that I had created of our wonderful honeymoon in Spain.

The doctor sat and listened intently until suddenly, it seemed like I had run out of things to say. The room suddenly fell deathly quiet, and I could feel my mind going into overdrive with panic, desperately trying to think of something else to say to break the silence. While the doctor continued to write in her notes, I began to feel like every muscle in my body had tensed up. As the doctor looked up from her notes through her little round glasses, I felt a strong wave of uneasiness rush through my body. The doctor suddenly seemed to be studying my tense face.

As she continued to observe my body language, I felt like the doctor was staring deep into my soul. I could sense that she knew that something was wrong. Yet I did not expect the doctor's next question.

An Emotional Diagnosis
"How's your sex life, Rachel?" she inquired, suddenly sounding more like a therapist than a family doctor. *Busted!* Panic-stricken, my body shook from the inside with the sudden rush of adrenaline that now circulated. *Why would she ask me such a question? Did she know?* I had now unexpectedly lost control of the situation.

As I'd sat in the doctor's office, I had tried to avoid divulging my shameful secret. The doctor's direct question about my sex life had caught me off guard, and suddenly, I found myself bursting into floods of tears.

Everything inside of me wanted to run away, but I knew that I desperately needed help. Part of me felt a sense of relief that the doctor had directly asked me about my sex life. While trying to choke back the tears, I tried to explain to the doctor that I could not have sex. Unexpectedly, the doctor gave me a warm and reassuring smile, along with a big box of tissues that seemed to quickly turn into a mountain of wet and disintegrated mush.

"Rachel, you have a condition called vaginismus."

"Excuse me? I have what?" I replied, looking confused.

The doctor paused and sat slowly back in her chair, as if contemplating how she could best explain why I had been struggling to have sex. With reassurance she explained, "Rachel, you have a condition that makes the muscles in your vagina go into a spasm. It's like having a panic attack, but the panic attack occurs in your vagina. Now, no one really understands why this happens, but research has shown that between 1 and 17 percent of women experience some type of sexual pain or vaginismus, and around two in every thousand women worldwide have some form of vaginismus."

I would learn that the Diagnostic and Statistical Manual of Mental Disorders (DSM-5) defines vaginismus, Genito-Pelvic Pain Disorder/Penetration Disorder, as "a persistent involuntary spasm that interferes with penetration, making it impossible, and considers any penetration, including insertion of tampons, finger, or difficulty with gynecological exams to be painful."[1] There is substantial research and literature indicating that there is little evidence that vaginismus is *only* caused by a muscle spasm. Vaginismus is thus defined as a woman merely having difficulty with full penetrative sexual intercourse. Certain scholars have even suggested that vaginismus can occur when the woman even anticipates that any object will penetrate her, including the smallest of objects such as a Q-tip.

Not Alone
"You mean to say that there are other women like me?" I said with disbelief, as I sat back in my chair, shocked. Only this morning I had held the belief that I was the only woman in the world who could not achieve sex. Now I had discovered that as many as two in every one thousand women could possibly be experiencing the same hellish nightmare as me.

She went on to explain that it appears that vaginismus is a condition affecting women all over the world, although many cases have been underdocumented, primarily due to the shame many women feel when admitting that they experience sexual pain. It is certainly understandable how so many women do not feel that they can talk about such a topic. In Western society, discussing issues concerning an inability to perform sexually often appears to be strictly taboo. It is acceptable for us to talk about drug addiction, alcohol problems and anxiety disorders. However, talking openly about sexual disorders is frequently deemed inappropriate. Even healthcare professionals find it

---

1 American Psychiatric Association, *Diagnostic and Statistical Manual of Mental Disorders*, 5th ed., (Arlington, Virginia: 2013), https://doi.org/10.1176/appi.books.9780890425596.

challenging to talk openly about sexual disorders. This is often due to a lack of comfort with and education on the subject.

Although I still had no one to talk to or confide in, I no longer felt so alone. My family doctor had somehow managed to figure out my shameful secret in all of ten minutes. Thank God that she had, because if she had not been educated in the subject of vaginismus, I might have remained naïve forever as to the reasons why I found it impossible to have sex. The doctor informed me that many women hide vaginismus for years, and some women even go their whole lives choosing not to seek help.

"Rachel, I have honestly seen women sitting in that very same chair you are sitting in right now, who have been suffering for over thirty years before they even decide to ask for help. You have a head start in dealing with this disorder, Rachel."

Hope of a Cure
"So, are you telling me that vaginismus is curable?" I asked, still gulping back tears, while the pile of wet disintegrated tissues continued to grow.

"Of course, it is curable, Rachel! I will arrange to see you over the next few weeks, and we will get you using dilators for around six weeks, and you should be cured. Dilators are around 99 percent effective," she continued reassuringly. The doctor seemed to allude to my condition as being a physical issue that could be cured by simply retraining my vaginal muscles with dilators.

I left that office believing that my vaginismus would be a simple fix, as it was a physical complaint. However, I later discovered that vaginismus is caused by both physical and psychological factors and although the doctor had addressed the physical aspects, she had failed to address the psychological part of my condition. Consideration of my upbringing and the shame I carried related to sex were not discussed, so at this point I was not aware of the psychological aspect of my condition that needed to be addressed.

I left the doctor's office with a sense of hope and relief that finally everything would turn out okay. I walked home through the old, cobbled streets as fast as I could to tell David the news. As soon as I entered our small college apartment, David could immediately see the glimmer of hope and relief buried underneath my puffy, bloodshot eyes. As I excitedly shared the words of the doctor with David, I could see the glimmer of hope and relief in his face. Finally, I had found an answer and a potential cure for this nightmare that we had been forced to live.

"Wow, Rachel! You need to get on the internet right now and order those dilators," David insisted, while he set up the laptop.

As I excitedly searched the web for dilators, I smiled and said, "So six weeks from now we will be able to have sex!"

After I placed my order for dilation treatment, I spent endless hours on the internet researching vaginismus. Finally, I had found a label for the embarrassing disorder that I had found myself inflicted with. But what did vaginismus actually mean?

Definition of Vaginismus

Vaginismus appears to be both a psychological and a physiological disorder. The brain sends out a message to the cognitions, emotions and behavioral responses that intercourse is going to be painful. This is a full-system response. The vaginal muscles then react by creating a powerful spasm that allows nothing to penetrate the vagina. This spasm is the body's way of creating a protective reflex to what the brain perceives to be a threat. The spasm may involve any of the vaginal muscles, and while the "PC" (pubococcygeus muscle) may be in spasm, the entry muscle to the vagina, known as the bulbocavernosus, is the muscle most frequently affected by the spasm. "The reflex causes the muscles in the vagina to tense involuntarily, which makes any form of vaginal penetration, including full sexual intercourse, painful or impossible."[2] Often a woman will describe her attempts at intercourse to be "like hitting a brick wall."

One question that had continued to run through my mind was, what occurred first, the fear of penetration or the pain caused by penetration? When someone is trapped during a violent storm with nowhere to hide, they are hardly going to be relaxed when they have another similar experience. If a woman suffers pain every time she attempts sexual intercourse or any kind of penetration, it is understandable that she is going to fear these experiences.

---

2 Lori Smith, "What you need to know about vaginismus," *Medical News Today*, February 13, 2018, https://www.medicalnewstoday.com/articles/175261.

But it could also be argued that the belief that penetration and sex are going to be painful could actually be causing the pain, since the woman's beliefs trigger a tensing of the muscles. It is also important to note that the partners of women suffering with vaginismus can also develop a fear or aversion toward sex. The constant rejection from their partner can leave them feeling like they have an aversion toward sex with that particular person. This is like a conditioned response.

Vaginismus was not a term I had been familiar with nor a disorder that I had heard anyone ever openly talk about. As I sat in front of the computer into the early hours of the morning, my eyes slowly began to droop. I had managed to exhaust myself with the hours of researching my newly diagnosed problem. *Who am I trying to kid? I am a freak, and that is all there is to it,* I thought. As my eyes drooped and became heavier, I could no longer fight the tiredness. I felt my head hit the computer as I drifted deeper and deeper into sleep. As I lay asleep, I heard the smash of my coffee cup as it fell to the floor. Barely able to open my eyes, I could see the coffee seeping into the cracks of the hardwood floor.

Overwhelmed by exhaustion, I attempted to lift my head in response to the crash of the mug, but my eyes could no longer stay open. Hours of searching the internet had left me with little understanding of why I had vaginismus. As I drifted into a deep sleep, I could feel my black cat Jasper nudging me and purring, as if he were trying to say that it was time to go to bed. After that, I drifted further and further into dreamland until I felt David's hand on my shoulder.

"Rachel, Rachel, wake up!" David stood over me and continued to shake me to wake me up. Failing to receive a response from me, he continued to insist that I wake up.

"Rachel! It's 4 a.m. and you need to come to bed."

With a gasp, I awoke from my sleep and frantically tried to gain control of my breathing. I could still feel my heart beating so fast that it felt like it would explode.

"Rachel, what's wrong? Are you okay?" David pulled me toward him in an attempt to try to calm me. Kissing me gently on the forehead, he told me that everything was going to be okay.

"No, no, it's not going to be okay, David! It should never have turned out this way."

As I tried to regain control of my breathing, I choked back my tears and asked, "How did we end up here, David? Why did this have to happen to us?"

David let out a big sigh as he realized that he had begun to play the role of counselor again. "I don't know, Rachel, but we will get through this, I know we will. It's going to be okay; I promise. Now come on, let's go to bed." David grabbed hold of my hand and pulled me toward the bedroom. "I promise, Rachel, we will get through this."

When I awoke the next morning, I continued my quest to find out more about what had caused me to suffer this bizarre disorder. There are two types of vaginismus, primary and secondary. With primary vaginismus, a woman has never been able to tolerate vaginal penetration of any kind due to an involuntary spasm of the muscles in the vagina. A woman suffering from secondary vaginismus has previously been able to have sexual intercourse without any difficulties, but then due to factors such as childbirth, trauma, rape or domestic violence, discovers that she is no longer able to tolerate any vaginal penetration.[3] A woman who has been subjected to a rough gynecological examination where she has felt out of control, could similarly fall victim to secondary vaginismus.

Literature also supports evidence of women experiencing situational vaginismus, where they may have no difficulties participating in a gynecological examination but may remain unable to have sexual intercourse with their partner. It is unclear what causes the woman to be unable to tolerate penetration, since it is difficult to distinguish between whether a muscle spasm in the vagina causes the pain experienced by many sufferers or whether the pain causes the spasm of the vagina.[4] Women who are suffering with vaginismus will often complain of a burning sensation in the vagina and surrounding areas, before or after penetration. It seems that this burning pain can occur not only with sexual intercourse, but also even during the insertion of a tampon or just a finger. Some cases of vaginismus are so severe that even the insertion of a Q-tip appears to be impossible.

Some women can have such severe vaginismus that they will elevate their buttocks, clamp their thighs and retreat whenever any kind

---

[3] Tamara Melnik and Oswaldo M. Rodrigues Jr., "Vaginismus is ruining sex. Research must move beyond penetration," *Evidently Cochrane*, accessed April 7, 2017, https://www.evidentlycochrane.net/vaginismus-ruining-sex/.
[4] "Vaginismus: Women Who Can't Have Intercourse," *HealthyPlace*, accessed December 6, 2008, https://www.healthyplace.com/sex/female-sexual-dysfunction/vaginismus-women-who-cant-have-intercourse.

of penetration is perceived. They are so severely affected by vaginismus that they often sweat, vomit and generally experience severe nausea. The fear of penetration is so severe that without sedation, these women could not be penetrated, even with the smallest of objects.

Why Me?
As I continued to read through the research on vaginismus and discuss my findings with David, I tried to define my own experience of vaginismus. David stood drawing in the kitchen while he listened to his music. He often drew and traced words and created poems about life that were very philosophical and of a political nature. It was a hobby that allowed him to escape reality for a while.

"The only way I can describe it is that it feels as if my vagina has a mind of its own. In my head, I want so desperately to have sexual intimacy, but for some reason my vagina is saying no. Why, David? Why would my vagina choose to say no to such a wonderful experience? I just don't understand," I asked with a frustrated tone.

"I don't know, Rachel. I wish I had the answer to all of this. I really do. It makes no sense, no sense at all." He put down his pencil and sat down on the couch next to me. David had found himself seeking an answer to the "why" question as much as I did, but he knew enough about life to know that sometimes we will never know the reasons why things happen.

"The doctor described it as if my vagina was scared, or experiencing a panic attack, whenever it perceived that anything would penetrate it. I just don't understand why it had to happen to us. We have always been good people and we obediently waited to have sex, and then this happens! I feel so cheated, David!"

Grabbing hold of my hand, David replied, "I know, Rachel. All my life I have felt like I have been constantly battling to stay afloat. From an abusive childhood to a life of homelessness and addiction, and I finally escape all that and now this—a sexless marriage."

Tears began to sting my eyes as I agreed with David. "I'm so sorry, David. You don't deserve this."

David quickly shot back with a serious and assertive tone, "No, Rachel! *We* don't deserve this! This is not your fault, and you must accept that this is not your fault. This problem stinks, but it is in no way your fault, okay?" David pulled me into his arms as I sobbed uncontrollably.

"I'm so scared, David. What if this is what our life is going to be like from now on? What if we can't get through this, then what? I don't want to lose you, but I don't want us to live like this," I said, sobbing.

Keeping Silent
Like many other women, I figured that I must be the only woman in the world walking around with this horrific problem. I felt like overnight my life had gone from feeling "normal" to feeling like I had turned into an alien. I could not understand why this shameful condition had chosen to inflict me. It felt like I had woken up in the middle of a hellish nightmare. Surely this kind of thing only happened to the unfortunate character on a movie screen who had been created by someone's imagination.

How can this be happening to me? I thought. Isolated and alone, I still felt like the only woman in the world who could not have sex. I now knew that other women with vaginismus existed, but where were they?

I knew that even if other women like me did exist, it wouldn't take away my extreme sense of isolation and loneliness. Just like me, these women most likely did everything in their power to protect the slightest bit of dignity that they had left. I realized that my best friend could be experiencing vaginismus, and I wouldn't know. Thousands of women are experiencing vaginismus, but like me, they remain isolated and alone.

After returning to Bible college following our honeymoon, every day, David and I found ourselves surrounded by Christians. The faculty placed great expectations on David and me to fit the perfect picture of the "perfect, squeaky-clean Christian couple" who had no issues and possessed a constant positive attitude.

Confiding in anyone at the university about our shameful issue would have demolished our perfect pastor/leader potential in the eyes of the leaders of the church, who would have seen my fear, phobias and anxieties as a weakness. There had been many occasions that I had seen people shamed and seen as less for having mental health issues. The church had taught me this was a weakness and was not of God. I remember the extreme fear I had growing up believing that a lot of mental health concerns were caused by demons. I would sit in church and worry that I would be "found out" and that I would be humiliated by a demon being cast out from me. Looking back, these fears seem irrational, but witnessing people having demons cast out leaves an impression that cannot easily be shifted from a person's mind. It again returns to that deep sense of shame that seems to haunt me and that feeling of never being able to reach the expectations of the church. Sadly, even today the Christian church is not adequately educated around caring for those with mental health concerns. Thankfully, the expectations of God are different from the expectations of the church.

Many years later, I learned of pastors and leaders of the church who have struggled alone with anxiety, fear, mental health issues and suicidal tendencies, and sadly, they remined silent. That silence has destroyed the lives of many through the loss of good leaders and pastors who, like me, felt they could not disclose their weaknesses to the church or to their leaders. They feared being seen as not strong enough in their faith and losing their positions.

The secret of vaginismus became a heavy burden for both David and me, and we carried our burden silently for many years, too ashamed and too frightened of being humiliated. Every day, the secret of vaginismus ate away at my identity as a woman and at my faith and beliefs. There were days when I sat in the bath with a razor in my hand and tears streaming down my face.

When someone finds herself in the midst of a situation she cannot control and starts to see the devastation it is causing to those around her, suicide can seem the best option to end everyone's pain and not just her own.

To those outside of the situation, this may seem like an illogical belief, but for those who find themselves in the eye of the storm facing suicidal thoughts, it sometimes seems like the most logical and kind action to take. The thoughts of family being angry and upset seem to be outweighed by the thoughts that their families would eventually realize that being gone and ending everyone's misery would be a blessing.

At the time, David and I could only hope the dilators, soon to arrive, would help.

Seed for Thought

"Therefore, prepare your minds for action; be self-controlled; set your hope fully on the grace to be given you when Jesus Christ is revealed" (First Peter 1:13).

CHAPTER SEVEN

Newlywed, Constant Dread

*"Hope is being able to see that there is
light despite all of the darkness" —Desmond Tutu*

I stared down at the ugly, unfriendly looking, cold, hard, plastic dilators I had just received in the mail at the suggestion of my doctor. I thought back to what the doctor had said to me that day in the office. "At least 99 percent of women are able to be cured from vaginismus if they use the dilators on a daily basis," the doctor had explained as she peered over her round glasses. She provided me with instructions on how to use the dilators.

Although there were other treatments on the market that were still being discovered, such as physiotherapy, cognitive behavioral therapy and Botox treatment, I was not offered or informed of any of these treatments.

"You need to be using them for at least fifteen to twenty minutes per day if you want to have success," the doctor had said.

As I sat on my bed staring at the unfriendly looking piece of cold plastic, I wondered how this cold piece of plastic could possibly end the intolerable pain I experienced whenever I tried to have sex. I'd failed on countless occasions to manage to get a warm penis inside of me, which seemed a lot more naturally appealing than a piece of cold, hard plastic!

"Okay, I can do this," I muttered to myself. Jimi Hendrix music blared from the kitchen where David stood cooking up a storm. I knew I would have no interruptions for quite a while.

I picked up the smallest dilator and generously coated it with lubricant and lay back on the bed. I did my best to relax my buttocks and thighs, as I had been instructed by my doctor. As the tip of the dilator contacted the entrance of my vagina, all I could feel was the cold and wet plastic.

As I slowly tried to insert the dilator, I began to feel the familiar pain starting to sear through my vagina like stabbing knives. Thinking that the pain would be relieved as soon as I pulled the dilator out, I quickly removed it. I never thought that I would experience a tight burning pain upon removing the dilator. Catching my breath, I glanced over toward the biggest dilator.

If I can't get the smallest one in, then how am I supposed to get the biggest one in? This is not going to work! I had barely gotten the tip of the smallest dilator inside of me, and I had already experienced the pain that had become so familiar.

After battling for an hour, I left the bedroom feeling defeated and returned to the living room to watch television. David glanced around at me from our open kitchen and enthusiastically inquired, "Well? Did you use your dilators?"

"Yes, but it hurt to even get the smallest one inside of me, and it took forever to make any progress. I don't think this is going to work, David. The pain from the smallest dilator is just unbearable. It barely gets past the entrance before I have to take it back out. I just don't see how this is going to get better."

"You have to keep using them, Rachel. You can't expect this condition to just disappear overnight. It is going to take a lot of hard work and determination on your part."

Discouraging Times

Our relationship had gone from being romantic and in love, to me taking on the role of the victim and David becoming my personal counselor. Often, he would find himself trying to encourage and counsel me through times where I just wanted to give up hope. This placed great strain on our marriage, a marriage that was no longer full of laughter and fun. Our marriage had become one big heap of problems that felt like a treadmill that was going nowhere.

Somehow, we had to try to work through these difficulties together, one step at a time. The added pressure of both of us studying for a degree in theology, the constant flow of church services, and not being able to share our marital issues with anyone else soon started to affect my mental health, which had started to deteriorate and affect other parts of my life.

* * *

"No! No! Oh, God…no. Please, no!" I screamed out into the pitch-black bedroom as I hysterically sat up in bed, clutching my chest and desperately gasping to catch my breath. David quickly switched on the light.

"Rachel, what's happening? It 3:15 in the morning! Did you have a nightmare?" David asked, while looking dazed from being suddenly woken from his sleep.

"I…I…can't breathe, and my heart is pounding!"

I jumped out of bed and began to pace up and down the bedroom, desperately trying to gain control over the thoughts that I would die. Night after night, this occurred and night after night, David consoled me. These panic attacks continued to haunt me every night for years.

"Why, God? Why are You torturing me like this? What did I do to deserve this?" I screamed. As the panic dwindled, I found myself left feeling exhausted and raging with anger that I had never experienced before. For the first time in my life, I had become angry toward God.

After my countless pleas for God to help me—to send me a miracle or to cure me—I'd begun to feel as if the heavens were deathly silent. As the panic continued to haunt me month after month, I began to find myself becoming bitter and angry toward the god I had begun to believe had let me down.

Feeling Cheated

I thought back to the big dreams I had while at Bible school: of David and me working together to help those who had become disadvantaged or who were suffering. I suddenly realized that I had become one of the disadvantaged and a person who was suffering, and it seemed so lonely and as if there was no one available who could truly understand our pain. For the first time in my life I had begun to feel stuck, like I was drowning in quicksand. It seemed no matter how hard I fought, nothing was working and I started to see no hope for our marriage. I thought back to the memories that I had at Bible school where I envisioned David sharing his testimony and me singing and offering words of encouragement. I had envisioned a church without walls where we would meet people where they were, but now it seemed that the dreams I had were slowly being taken from me and I was left with a sense of hopelessness. I remembered looking at other women in the college and thinking they were better than me. They seemed to have nothing holding them back.

I felt cheated by a god I had been taught from early childhood to follow. I was taught that he was a god who would never harm me and who loved me.

For the first time in my life, I found myself doubting the faith I had been raised to follow. I contacted pastors and attempted to talk with counselors, but no one really considered looking at the deeper psychological or emotional aspects of my condition until many years later. My success in overcoming vaginismus would have been more likely if I had received more seamless specialist interventions at the beginning of being diagnosed with my condition.

Trying to remain passionate in my studies about the Christian faith had become extremely challenging. I had begun to loathe the young women who surrounded me at college and who seemed to just calmly breeze around the college without a care in the world. There remained great emphasis on the expectations that the faculty had placed upon David and me to pray, actively worship and live out the character of good upstanding Christians who displayed no flaws or doubts about what they believed. Yet neither David nor I could bring ourselves to worship a god we felt abandoned by in our most desperate time of need.

I felt like nothing more than a fake. A fake woman, and now a fake Christian. I felt like my identity had begun to crumble like a dilapidated building. I had been left feeling empty and undesirable, with no positive prospects. I constantly asked myself the same question, over and over again: Who am I? From childhood, all I had ever wanted was to serve God.

Now I had been left doubting everything I had ever been taught about my beliefs. The place I had always perceived as a safe haven no longer felt safe and secure. If God is real, then how could He ignore my desperate cries for help? God had listened to my desperate pleas and tears of suffering, night after night, as I begged Him to take away the torture I was facing, and it seemed that He had chosen not to step in and remove the pain and suffering I was experiencing.

I became a professional at putting on a fake smile every day, as I knew that most people wouldn't be able to understand my pain. How could I expect people to understand a problem that I myself had never known existed until I became a victim of it myself? I also feared the sniggers and the sympathy I knew would make me feel even worse.

David and I continued fighting my inner demons by ourselves, and faithfully I kept my appointments for counseling and dilation treatment. The help I was receiving from counselors and doctors was very disjointed. I would see my family doctor, who focused heavily on dilation treatment, and the counselors tackled the surrounding issues of low self-esteem, not feeling like a woman and the guilt and shame of vaginismus. There were no doctors or counselors who focused on both aspects, which would have been more beneficial.

After much determination, I reached the fourth dilator out of the five. I saw this as a successful moment, even though it took me over an hour to get it only a quarter of the way in. The searing and burning pain became so unbearable that I quickly removed the dilator, feeling some deflation about my success.

Six-Week Mark
When the six-week mark arrived, I reflected on the assurance of the doctor that "around 99 percent of women will be cured with dilation treatment at around the six-week mark." I realized that I had now joined the 1 percent of women who did not respond to dilation therapy. Although I continued to turn up to the sessions with my doctor, I could sense that she, too, was slowly losing her hope that I would be cured.

As much as I had tried to make the dilator treatment work, I knew that this disorder had started to get the better of me. My mood deteriorated, and I began to gain weight from comfort eating. This seemed to be the only pleasure David and I had at this point in our lives. It was difficult to remain positive in what felt like a tornado that was slowly starting to rip my life to shreds, and it felt like I was unable to do anything to prevent the destruction it was causing. I had found myself amid circumstances that I could only relate to a violent storm I had no way of controlling.

While researching vaginismus, I began to learn that it was graded from mild to severe cases and that the disorder presented in many different shapes, sizes and forms. Like a tornado, this condition carved a deep and wide path of destruction, which for many resulted in damage to their identity as women, their relationship, their self-esteem and even their employment and social life. The shape, size and eventual landfall of a tornado determine what the effect of the tornado will be.

For example, an F5 tornado will cause severe damage to anything in its path, whereas the destruction of an F1 tornado has fewer dire consequences. However, even with an F1 tornado, if there are houses and people in its path, it is still possible that some level of devastation will occur and sometimes, for those closest to the storm, fatality results.

Similarly, a woman with a mild case of vaginismus could experience only mild destruction in her life, whereas a woman who has a severe Lamont level 5 vaginismus may suffer from extreme chaos and destruction that will permeate every aspect of her life. I only found out that I was a level 4 when I found a doctor who understood vaginismus, which was more than eleven years after I had been first diagnosed by my family doctor when we returned from our honeymoon.

Until this point, I had only been informed that I had vaginismus. When vaginal examinations were attempted, they were unsuccessful and left me feeling embarrassed and judged.

Tornado Levels
Like a tornado, vaginismus can be defined as having five different levels. In 1978, J.A. Lamont, a lecturer at McMaster University, claimed that

vaginismus could be divided into four different levels. Many years later a plastic surgeon named Peter Pacik developed the Lamont Scale further, adding level 5, and the scale is still referred to today.

1. Level one is classified as mild and can usually be resolved with simple reassurance.
2. Level two involves the woman having a noticeable spasm that remains during a pelvic exam, even after the woman has been reassured.
3. A woman with level three vaginismus will elevate her buttocks to avoid being examined.
4. If suffering from level four vaginismus, a woman will elevate her buttocks, clamp her thighs together, and retreat. (I was to discover that I was afflicted with level four vaginismus, and I did not discover this until I was diagnosed by a plastic surgeon in the US who specialized in vaginismus.)
5. In level five the woman may react by screaming, shouting, trembling, hyperventilating, shaking, vomiting or going unconscious or attempting to jump off a table.[5]

As each day passed, I felt David growing more and more distant and resentful toward me. He became more agitated, angry and withdrawn. My overwhelming sense of guilt continued to grow, and I constantly cried, wondering if David and I should stay together. I failed to understand why David had chosen to stay with me when he felt so trapped. Deep down, I knew David wanted to do right by me, but the cracks in our relationship had started to show.

The impact of vaginismus is not restricted to the women involved. Partners are also deeply affected. The impact of the condition is felt in multiple areas of the individual, severely affecting self-esteem, and can have devastating effects on the woman and all those around her.

For some, vaginismus involves fear regarding penetration and pain and can be similar to a phobia or a fear of injections. In relation to my

---

5 Peter T. Pacik, "Vaginismus: Review of Current Concepts and Treatment Using Botox Injections, Bupivacaine Injections, and Progressive Dilation with the Patient Under Anesthesia," Springer Science+Business Media, LLC and International Society of Aesthetic Plastic Surgery 2011. Published online 10 May 2011. https://www.vaginismusmd.com/wp-content/uploads/2011/09/ASPJ-Pacik-BTX-Vaginismus-2011-paper.pdf.

own journey with vaginismus, it seemed that there was an underlying and intense phobic reaction to penetration that caused me to experience physical pain. Although I had identified that my phobias were contributing to my disorder, I never confided in healthcare professionals about my phobias. I already felt like a freak and often had to explain my condition to many professionals, so confusing them about my phobias seemed too overwhelming, and no one ever asked.

One afternoon, David and I had been having another one of our heated arguments when he said, "I could get an annulment, you know; it's not right that we are living this way. How can I preach from the pulpit when my own life is a complete mess? I feel like a complete fake, Rachel, like we are living a lie!"

"But it's not our fault, David! It is not like I am doing this on purpose! Surely God understands that we cannot do the impossible."

David sighed and sat down, "I know that, Rachel, but don't you feel like a fake? Pretending that everything is okay and trying to help others and always giving the impression that we are the strong ones when clearly we're not."

As without fail I would start to cry, thinking about what we had been through and feeling powerless to stop what was happening to us and to our marriage.

"You know I would never leave you, Rachel. I'm just so frustrated with all of this and I don't know what to do or where to turn for help. I just feel like we are trapped, and no one seems to be able to help us."

Hearing David talk about abandoning our marriage when I was so early in the process of facing my disorder left me with a sense of mistrust. I felt an overwhelming sense of panic and all I could think about was the deep shame I felt and how even my family would judge me for failing at my marriage.

I had begun to hate myself, and my self-esteem was continuing to decline. When I looked at my reflection in the mirror, I no longer saw the happy, smiling Rachel I had known before getting married. Instead, I saw a guilt-ridden, unattractive, miserable-looking woman staring back at me.

I began to constantly worry that David would leave me and expose who I truly was. I was left feeling like I was a liar to all the people around me. It affected my friendships and the way I responded and interacted with family and even strangers. I no longer wanted to let people be close to me in case they found out my shameful and humiliating secret.

Feeling Like a Freak
Even though David had become romantically distant, he continued to console me. But often he would become angry whenever he listened to my constant expressions of low self-esteem and my continual rants of "I'm a freak."

Although I had been informed that around 1 percent of women had vaginismus by a doctor early in my diagnosis, part of me did not believe there were other women like me. *If there are other women like me, where are they? Who are they?*

It would have been so helpful to have had contact with other women like me. It may have prevented me from feeling so abnormal and perceiving myself as a freak of nature. I eventually found some online chat rooms where women discussed vaginismus, but it still never felt real to me. I could not even begin to imagine that there were other women who were like me.

Vaginismus felt like a horrible joke and part of me did not want to find other women like me as it was often easier to deny that something was wrong. I also felt so overwhelmed by how vaginismus was destroying my marriage that emotionally and socially I began to shut down. The only emotions I expressed were behind closed doors and were so extreme that they began to push David further away from me.

The daily effort David made in cooking my favorite dishes and bringing me cups of tea in bed assured me that David still loved me. But the daily guilt and shame had become unbearable and my constant fake smile to the world began to fade.

I began to sleep poorly. Every night I would wake up in the early hours of the morning with a pounding heart, thinking that God was not going to allow me to awaken from my sleep. I began to develop severe aversions to particular foods and found that I could no longer self-administer medications like I used to. A strong fear of dying had now developed, and every thought I had about my death involved either a tragic or torturous ending. This caused me to develop issues with taking any tablet, as I believed I would experience a severe allergic reaction and die. When I tried to take tablets, they became stuck in my throat, even with buckets of water to push them down. My self-esteem had become so low that I became fixated on thoughts about how I was destroying David's life.

I began to fear the consequences of destroying David's faith and the ministry that God had planned for him. I developed a strong belief that my sexual disorder had now become a hindrance to God's plan for our lives. If I didn't find a cure to my embarrassing problem soon, I was sure God would find a way to release David from the heartache and pain I was now causing him. Taking a simple medication became a nightmare. I would have full-blown panic attacks over the thought that I would have an anaphylactic allergic reaction and die. I struggled with the realization that David was having to suffer even more pain and suffering after he had fought so hard to overcome his homelessness and drug addictions.

Delusional Thoughts

One morning I awoke from my usual disturbed sleep, resting in bed but still half-asleep. I had never been a morning person, so it was not unusual for me to take a while to wake up. I could hear David moving around in the kitchen, making tea as he usually did. He knew that caffeine would be the quickest way to get me moving. I could hear him banging the cups down on the counter and the click of the kettle, and then I heard him stirring the tea.

Why was he stirring my tea? I thought. *I don't take sugar in my tea, so why would he stir it?* As I remained deep in thought, the bedroom door flung open.

"Morning," David said, smiling, as he placed the steaming hot cup of tea into my hands.

"Thanks," I said. I found myself suspiciously accepting the cup of tea from his hands and I placed it on the bedside table. A few minutes later I got out of bed and started to head toward the shower.

David sat in bed, looking puzzled at my sudden eagerness to get out of bed. "Are you not going to drink your tea, Rachel?" he asked.

"Yeah," I shouted down the hallway. "I'm just going to shower first."

I never did drink that tea, and I started to avoid drinking drinks that David had made for me. I always enjoyed David's cooking, but now

I found myself eagerly volunteering to cook and if David did cook, I watched his every move. Eventually David became suspicious of the constant refusal to drink his tea and one morning he decided to confront me.

Crying with shame and embarrassment, I replied, "I keep thinking that you're going to poison me!" I could see the shock and disbelief in David's facial expression.

With a shocked look on his face, he asked, "Why would you think I would do such a thing?" I knew from his facial expression that he was hurt by my lack of trust in him, but I couldn't shut off the thoughts starting to flood my mind that he was going to try to kill me. Even though I knew my thoughts were illogical, I could not switch the thoughts off and part of me knew he was struggling to stay strong.

David suggested I talk to the counselor about my phobias, but I felt too ashamed and was deeply worried that I would be given medications and sent to a mental hospital. Being mentally ill was again something that has and continues to be misunderstood by the church. I remembered witnessing many people with mental health disorders seeking help through prayer at the front of the church and then watching pastors shout and scream over them for demons to leave their bodies.

Every time I went to church, I started to panic, thinking that if I sought out prayer, they would do the same to me, especially if I confided in them about my phobias. David was overwhelmed by seeing his newly married wife falling apart at the seams, and he did not seem to know what to do to make things better.

I stood in the hallway in my pajamas and began to cry, knowing that David was getting exhausted with my constant crying. "Because I'm a freak, David! I'm messed up and I can't see why you would want to be with me anymore!"

David was now pacing up and down the bedroom, holding his head in confusion. Every day, it seemed that his wife was becoming more and more detached from reality, and still we wore our fake smiles and hid our devastation behind closed doors.

He quickly shot me a glance of disapproval and said, "So, you think I would stoop so low as trying to kill you? Why would I kill you, Rachel? You're my wife, and I married you because I loved you!" David yelled.

I could see that my low self-esteem and feelings of worthlessness and guilt were beginning to frustrate David. Every day he tried to stay strong, but often he said he felt like he had become a counselor rather than a lover. I continued to express my illogical thoughts, which were another burden for David to carry.

"If you divorced me, it would destroy your chances of ever becoming a minister," I said. "So, I guess in my head, I thought if you poisoned me and made it look like I died of natural causes, your name would be clear. You would be free from living this nightmare of a marriage and you wouldn't have to explain to anyone why you had decided to leave me."

David came to an abrupt halt with his pacing, sat down on the bed beside me, and sighed deeply. "Rachel, surely deep down you know I could never do something so terrible. I would never hurt you! I love you!" he said as he put his arms around me. "Things are no way near perfect, but I do still love you, Rachel!"

As I wiped the tears from my face, I tried to pull myself together. I often found that I was unable to speak because I was so distressed from crying, and after crying, I felt exhausted for the rest of the day. "I'm so sorry, David. I don't know where these thoughts are coming from, but they feel so real to me. I don't deserve to be alive, not when I am causing so much misery and pain."

Although I still believed that David would one day poison me, I found that having that conversation with him helped me tremendously. David had been right, deep down I did know that he would never hurt me. Yet I still continued to battle daily thoughts that David secretly wanted to get rid of me. I had never experienced constant thoughts that were so persistent. However, I soon realized that these negative thoughts were false delusions.

With a great deal of patience on David's part, I began to trust David again. But the deterioration in my mental health had left scars on our marriage that would take a long time to fade.

Lost

As the years flew by, David became worn down by the constant rejection and mistrust he felt from me. Vaginismus was like a cancer; it truly spread into every part of our lives and it destroyed my self-esteem, damaged the intimacy in our relationship, and destroyed our spiritual life and my mental health. It had begun to affect our physical health too. Every day became a battle to keep going, and friends couldn't understand why both David and I had become so distant from them. Every day was a battle to just survive daily tasks and live with the guilt and the thoughts of causing so much misery to a husband who didn't deserve to suffer again in his life.

Even though we continued with our ongoing battle, David and I traveled to Canada for three months to sing and testify about David's release from drug addiction. Many people were blessed by David's amazing battle and recovery from a life of homelessness and drug addiction. Yet we still carried our unanswered prayer and hidden devastation of being unable to consummate our marriage and remaining childless.

We had been married for around two years, and David and I had hoped to start a family and settle down together. I wanted a boy and a girl, and I imagined our son being like David, strong-willed, cheeky and full of life. I hoped to have a daughter who would be caring toward others and who would follow in my footsteps and sing and enjoy acting and have a creative flare. I dreamt of us going to places as a family, such as the seaside or the park, and our children spending time with their grandparents. Our short-lived itinerant ministry as evangelists was soon shattered after we realized that our issues had become more serious and difficult to ignore.

David and I began to feel like fakes, testifying to a release from drug addiction, which remained the truth, but we were now battling a bizarre problem that was not being resolved by our constant prayer. On reflection, if we had been honest about our bizarre struggles, it would have further emphasized the testimony of David's recovery from drug addiction. There are many addicts who get through the process of recovery only to return to what they know when life becomes tough. Clearly, God had released David from his drug addiction and was giving him the strength to get through the pain and suffering he was experiencing without the need to return to his drug use.

Reclaiming Privacy
Every day I would feel on edge with the fear that David would confide in someone. Staying in different people's homes across Canada left us

feeling like we were always guests without privacy or time to ourselves. Often we found ourselves counseling others while we continued to battle our own doubts and questions as to why God had not chosen to end our suffering. After hours of involvement in ministry and counseling, we found minimal time left to spend with each other and little privacy available to address or talk freely about our unresolved issue.

One Sunday afternoon, David and I sat outside on the steps of a church in Calgary. Confused and exhausted, David and I had begun to discuss our future. Living out of a suitcase and bouncing from one house to another and continually having to stay strong was becoming too much for both of us.

"I don't know how much longer we can live like this, Rachel." David's head hung low with defeat. Being involved in Christian ministry had conveniently allowed us both to live in a world of denial and not address our problem. We crowded our lives with helping others and lived the life of expected positivism that the church expected from its leaders.

We went from church to church, sharing our testimony and singing, and became involved with youth and children's camps where we helped with activities. We spent many evenings talking with pastors and their families at their homes where we stayed. David was often called to talk with a young person who had become involved with drugs, and he shared his life story.

It was a time full of wonderful memories, and many lives were impacted by our ministry, but every day was a struggle trying to keep our heads above water with what we were battling in our marriage. I worried that our problem would never get resolved as we had no privacy as a couple. During the day we never stopped and if we were not visiting people, preaching or singing, we would be involved in manual duties around the church.

Neglecting our own marital problems and centering our efforts solely on church ministry left us with a marriage that was beginning to fall apart. After hours of discussion, we realized that we needed to leave the itinerant side of ministry and return home. Continually moving from place to place every few nights and never having time alone and always being in different people's homes prevented us from moving forward in resolving my vaginismus.

On our return home to the United Kingdom, we had no jobs or a place to live. For six months we lived with my mom and dad, which was not ideal and allowed for minimal privacy. We spent half of our time arguing in whispers, trying to hide our humiliating problem. My parents noticed how tense and angry David had become and were concerned that our problem had not been resolved. I begged David not to tell my parents that our struggles continued. Returning to England had been the right decision, but having no career, no place to live and not even a car left us with little independence as a married couple.

After six months, David was offered the position of assistant pastor in a nearby city church. Excited about the prospect of reclaiming our independence as a married couple and serving God, David accepted the job. With little money to our name, David managed to raise enough money to buy a small red Volkswagen Golf that got us to the city in the United Kingdom where we would take on the role of assistant pastor and wife.

We were now living in a busy city and David and I could only hope and pray that taking on the role of assistant pastor and wife would be the right path that would lead us to success in addressing our issue.

Seed for Thought
"Your word is a lamp to my feet and a light for my path" (Psalm 119:105).

CHAPTER EIGHT

The Valley of the Dry Bones

"You begin to fly when you let go of self-limiting beliefs and allow your mind and aspirations to rise to greater heights." —Brian Tracy

As I sat in our bedroom waiting for David to return home from church, I realized that it had been almost five months since we arrived in the big city. We lived with Florence, an eighty-five-year-old lady in the church, while we were in the process of purchasing our first house. When David and I were informed that we would be working in an inner-city church, it all seemed so exciting and we were thrilled.

As we entered the busy streets of the city with our old red Volkswagen, I looked around at the run-down buildings and the people walking around aimlessly. As we entered further into the center of downtown, there seemed to be more Indian takeout restaurants than there were houses. However, David and I adored Indian food, so the constant smell of Indian cuisine was not a problem.

Meeting Expectations
David and I did all we could to try to be the perfect committed pastor and wife. We constantly jumped through the hoops and fulfilled all the high expectations placed on us both. Yet our sex life continued to

suffer, and our problem remained unresolved. With all the stress happening around us, it just seemed easier to ignore the serious problem with our marriage. Although we had returned to the United Kingdom and taken on a stable role at a church, it still felt like we had no time to ourselves. David would spend most of his day visiting people at the hospital and at their homes. Then at night he would be expected to show up at prayer meetings, youth meetings and home groups, which again took away a lot of the time we had together. The expectations for us to both perform well were extremely high. There was a poster on the wall of the church entrance that said, "Do or die." David constantly felt that our lives were crowded with doing, and there was not enough time to stop and address our problems.

David was starting to feel the stress of the isolation, and I constantly begged him not to share our humiliating problem with the church leaders or parishioners. David described himself as feeling like a fraud when he preached. He always had a love and a passion for reading and sharing the Scripture, but his joy of sharing and encouraging others to trust in God had been lost. Unable to resolve the issue in his own marriage had left David feeling like he was providing people with false hope.

A friend told us that we should use stumbling blocks as stepping-stones and that there would be times in our lives when we would feel as if we were being crushed. He also said that God would not allow us to suffer more than we could handle.

David and I felt crushed and trapped in a place where we could see no answer or way out. I remembered someone once saying to me that the big truths only become applicable when big problems occur. Although we felt like we were being crushed, God truly was at work behind the scenes. When challenges occur, it is not until we look back at where we have come from that we truly see what God was trying to teach us. I spent nearly every Sunday sitting alone in church, constantly thinking about my marriage and trying to work out why we had been afflicted with this problem.

As other people around me sang, worshiped and danced, I did everything in my power to hold back the tears. Everyone seemed so happy, blessed and unburdened. I knew that if I could overcome my difficulties and concentrate, I would have a lot of talent and creativity to share. Yet

I felt trapped and unable to move on with my life. My life felt like it was stuck on a merry-go-round, or like *The Truman Show* where my life had become one big setup or joke.

Ultimate Betrayal

One day was not like any other day for David because he had decided that he was going to confide in the senior pastor about our situation. It had been almost three years now that we had been struggling alone. He knew that he had exhausted himself trying to stay strong and he needed a listening ear. As David remained deep in thought, the office door swung open and James, the senior pastor, rushed in with his briefcase in hand and sat down.

"Morning, David," James said with his usual serious tone, as he unlocked his briefcase and turned on his computer.

"Morning, James. Would I be able to talk to you about something? There's just something that is weighing heavy on my thoughts at the moment and I just…" David was suddenly cut off by the church secretary bringing James his morning tea and biscuits.

"Thank you, Pam, you're so good to me," James said while winking and smiling at the secretary. "So, David, you were saying?"

After checking that the door was securely closed, David took a deep breath and began to share his story with James. He explained the "condition" I had and how we had been unable to consummate our marriage for the last few years.

"I don't know what to do, James. I feel so exhausted from battling with this condition every day. I keep waiting for things to get better, but they don't. Rachel seems to be getting more bitter, angry and depressed. I just don't know what to do anymore."

As James listened, David saw that he was having some difficulty understanding whether such an issue was possible. He replied, "So you're saying that you and Rachel have not had sex since you gotten married?"

"Yes, that's correct," David said, feeling somewhat humiliated by his confession.

"Well, my advice to you would be that you need to leave her."

"Leave her? But surely that would be deemed as being wrong in God's eyes?" David said. He could not believe his ears. His senior pastor was advising him to divorce his wife—this was not the advice he had expected to receive. As David sat quietly, stunned by his senior pastor's advice, James continued.

"You and Rachel have not consummated your marriage in almost three years, so technically you are living a lie," James insisted. "Things are not going to get any better in a situation like this. If I were you, I would end it now and move on."

David sat silently as he tried to process the unexpected advice James had just given to him. "I don't think you understand. I love Rachel and the last thing I want to do is to leave her. No, I won't leave her! I need to find someone who can help Rachel overcome this disorder."

James drank the remainder of his tea and finished the cookies, deep in thought. "There is a Christian counselor I know who may be able to help."

"I will try anything, James, anything at all to try to save my marriage," David pleaded.

"Okay then, I will arrange for you to see a Christian counselor here at the church. Hopefully, she can help resolve this situation sooner rather than later." James picked up the phone and began dialing the number for the Christian counselor.

Icing on the Cake
Back at our home, I sat on my old creaky single bed, waiting for David to return. I flicked through the paper, dreaming of the day when we would finally get the keys to the house we could call our own. *It would be so nice to have our own house and have a cat and some children running around,* I thought. I had always wanted to be a mother, and there seemed to be something magical about becoming pregnant with a child created with the person you loved most in the world. It seemed to be the icing on the cake that made a couple a family, and I deeply desired that.

I sat on the side of the bed and stared at the dark green, old-fashioned walls. As I looked around the room, I stared at the old green curtains and the old-fashioned wallpaper and the antique furniture. I wondered if I would ever be able to overcome the vaginismus and become a mom. I knew it would make David so happy to become a dad. He had been through so much that it had become a deep desire of mine to provide him with a loving family he could call his own. As I looked at the houses, I wiped the sweat forming on my forehead. The room smelled musty and like mothballs. The fan in the corner of our bedroom was running on top speed but failed to cool the room down. As I walked over to the windows to try to open them, I heard David coming up the stairs.

"Only me," David shouted from the top of the stairs. A few seconds later, the bedroom door opened, and David flopped onto his single bed next to mine.

With frustration, I continued to fight with the window to try to let some air into the room.

"Oh, it's no use. Seriously, why would someone think it was a good idea to paint the windows shut!" I said as I sat down on my bed and turned toward David. "So how did your day at the office go?"

There was an awkward pause before David answered and then without warning he quickly blurted out, "I told James about our problem. I'm so sorry, Rachel."

"You did what!" I screeched with my eyes suddenly wide with panic. I could feel my heart beginning to pound with fear as the adrenaline rushed around my body.

"I had to tell someone, Rachel! I am so tired of dealing with this situation alone!" David yelled.

"What did he say?" I asked hesitantly, not really wanting to know the answer. I knew that James, like many other people, would have judged me.

"Trust me, Rachel; you really don't want to know what he said."

I already knew that I would be deemed a disappointment, so it was no surprise that the reaction David received to his plea for help was a negative one. However, I did not expect our pastor to advise my husband to divorce me. David never did go into detail about what had been said, and I was not sure that I felt strong enough to hear what had been said.

Finally, he said, "He wants us to go for counseling with a lady in the church, Rachel. He thinks it might help."

"She won't understand, David! She won't even know what vaginismus is! Believe me, it's a complete waste of time and energy," I shouted.

"Look, we don't have many choices here, okay? So we are going to give it a try!" David said.

Christian Counseling

Unfortunately, David and I soon realized that the counselor truly did not understand "the nature of the beast," vaginismus. But counseling did seem to bring awareness of some of my root behaviors that seemed to have led to the vaginismus occurring.

This started to help me understand that vaginismus was not something that had decided to just choose me to inflict. There had been a set of learned behaviors and stories that I had taught myself about sex. To make matters even worse, we eventually found out that all our confidential counseling information had been exchanged between the "counselor" and Pastor James. He now knew everything about us, even personal information about my life.

On our third wedding anniversary, it was hard to believe we had been married for three years. The counseling sessions felt like a mirror being placed in front of me, and I could now clearly see the situation and the surrounding circumstances. I started to gain some insight and self-awareness into my situation. I began to realize my need to have full control of every aspect of my life.

My need for control went far beyond a need to be in control of sex, but it affected my need to control what entered my body with medications and food, what health treatment I would accept, what car journeys I would or would not undertake, and what type of friends and relationships I would accept. My need to remain in control seeped into every aspect of my life, and the roots were deep. I started to realize that I was allowing fear to control me, and it was robbing me of living life. I had thought I was in control of my life, yet I was not in control of my life at all—fear was what was in control of me. Vaginismus was merely the tip of the iceberg, and what lay beneath my disorder was much more than I had ever realized.

Fear of Death

Within the first few months of getting married, I had started to experience panic attacks that became more frequent and intense as I undertook the counseling sessions. One night, I was jolted awake from a deep sleep with a racing heart and an impending sense of doom.

I often screamed out in panic and called for David as I sat bolt upright in bed, clutching my chest and feeling like I was going to die. It was not until a few weeks later that I realized I had a fear of death. I had once heard a guest speaker at a conference talk about anxiety, phobias and fears specifically related to a severe fear of death. During the talk, I began to feel hot and flustered, like I was beginning to panic. He had obviously hit a nerve, as what he was sharing on this topic was really starting to affect me in a physical way.

He said people who experienced an extreme fear of death had often been abused by someone with power in the church, such as a priest. I had no idea why I was reacting the way I was. To my knowledge, I had never suffered any sexual or physical abuse from the church. I had obsessively studied my childhood on countless occasions without learning anything about why I had vaginismus.

I couldn't understand why I had such an aversion to sex if I had not been sexually abused or raped. The fact that I had such a strong physical reaction to hearing the lecturer talk about the church and anxiety left me thinking that the strong views and negative messages from the church surrounding sex had left me somewhat frightened. Even though I dug deep through my memories, I could not remember any abuse from my past.

Later that week, David and I decided to go visit my parents. My parents were a sixty-minute drive from the city where we were living. As we walked around the local town before walking to my parents' house, David confided that he had been feeling particularly flat because everywhere he looked, all he saw were couples holding hands, families walking around with their children, and women walking around looking sexy and confident. David confided that he felt guilty for looking at other women and thinking about sex. He felt extremely guilty for having such thoughts about other women. As David began to open up about how he felt, it started to resurrect all of the insecurities, fears and feelings of failure, guilt and rejection that plagued me daily.

Breaking Point

It seemed that whenever we started talking about vaginismus, it always entered the same vicious circle. David talked about his feelings of frustration, anger and feeling trapped, and I lapsed into the feelings of guilt, fear, despair and feeling like a total freak of nature. We had no one else, apart from counselors and professionals, to whom we could talk about our feelings around vaginismus, which then became a trigger point for both of us.

Whenever we reached a point of intensity, we ended up shouting at each other, which then led to opening the floodgates to the high potential for marital crisis. It always seemed easier to just deny that we had a problem at all and avoid this whole part of our marriage altogether, thinking it would become less painful. Nearly every time we attempted to communicate about our issue, it either ended up in us arguing or me shutting myself in the bathroom.

Sometimes the intensity and pain of what David and I were facing was just too much to bear, and the bathroom seemed to become a safe haven for me, a place that would force the conversation to end and the intense pain to stop. Part of me thought it was safer to run away than to keep on arguing and feeling like the arguments would just lead to us failing in our marriage. If I hid in the bathroom, all the horrible mess and the intensity and pain would be gone.

After having time to compose myself again and for David to go and chill out with some music, all our pain and suffering was conveniently forgotten again, until the next time either David or I decided to face our denial and avoidance.

As David and I sat in my parents' lounge on the couch, we attempted to hold it all together and engage in normal conversation. However, the cracks were starting to show through, and I could sense that yet another breaking point was looming in our marriage. David had decided to ignore my usual pleas with him for secrecy and, against my will, he decided to confide in my mom about our ongoing problem. This was the second time David had ignored my pleas to remain quiet. Although deep down I knew that David longed to find a solution and someone to share his pain, it did not outweigh the feelings of guilt, inadequacy and shame that I felt, especially at the thought of my parents realizing that I was the cause of so much pain and heartache for David and was abnormal compared with other women around me.

I knew part of me craved someone I could confide in who would help me find a solution without leaving me feeling judged. But it seemed like no one understood, even doctors or church leaders, so I felt that confiding in my parents would only bring more shame rather than a solution, which I knew they did not have.

As I sat and watched as my mom awkwardly and quietly listened to David's utter frustration about us living with vaginismus, I began to break down in tears. I could sense my mother's shock when she heard from David how we had still been unable to consummate our marriage. Mom attempted, as best as she knew how, to understand and offered some suggestions on how we might overcome the pain. A part of me felt a great sense of relief that my parents knew that David and I were still struggling. Yet at the same time, I felt an overwhelming sense of humiliation, shame and embarrassment.

Every time David and I gained enough courage to speak to a professional or someone in authority about our marital issues, whether it was a doctor, nurse, vicar or even our senior pastor, they did not know how to help us. Instead, they gave wrong advice or uncaringly said that I was "frigid" and "just needed to relax." It seemed that more and more people were becoming aware of my humiliating problem and for what? No one seemed to have the answer. I was doomed for life.

Breaking Through

On many occasions, I packed my bags to leave my husband and as I packed, David would unpack and he would continue to say that he loved me. David did not want to give up on our marriage, and neither did I, but I was emotionally exhausted from trying to fix a problem that seemed to be impossible.

We continued with our counseling at the church, even though we knew that the counselor disclosed a lot of our personal information to Pastor James, because we were desperate for something to help.

After a few counseling sessions, David and I decided to attempt intercourse again. One afternoon, David managed to get inside of me, but the pain was unbearable, and he only managed a few seconds before I began pleading with him to stop.

"David, you did it! You managed to get inside of me!" I said with tears of joy.

"But I was barely inside of you, Rachel, and I could see the pain in your eyes. It shouldn't be this difficult," David replied.

"But it's still progress, David. We have never been able to get that far before."

"Yeah, but it feels unusually tight and uncomfortable, Rachel. It doesn't feel right and how can I even move around when you feel so much pain from me barely being inside of you?" David was grateful for the small step of progress we had just made, but he knew we still had a long way to go before we could have sex.

At that moment, although it had been painful, I genuinely believed that everything would be okay.

Breaking Away

Shortly thereafter, David had to attend a conference for three days with the church. David explained to Pastor James the importance of needing time away from church duties to establish and maintain what had taken us years to achieve and asked if he could miss the conference. The answer was a straight *no*. That evening, David packed his bag and left to attend the three-day church conference, and our small window of opportunity for a breakthrough quickly disappeared.

Desperate to maintain my success, I attempted to continue with dilation treatment in the hope that David and I could pick up where we left off when David returned home from the conference. However, my success with dilation treatment had remained unchanged from when I had initially tried it. After about an hour of pushing against what felt like a brick wall, I finally managed to get the tip of the dilator inside of me. The next day, I was back to square one again. Nothing had changed from the times I had previously tried to work with dilation treatment. When David returned home from his conference, we attempted sex again. Sadly, we soon found out that we were back to square one.

While David continued to work as assistant pastor at the church, I made the decision to return to school to complete my nurse's training. While making conversation with Pastor James, David shared my plans with him.

"You have to be careful, David! You don't want Rachel being around all those doctors! This isn't good!" It seemed strange that he would make such a comment when he was fully aware of the difficulties I had been facing with sexual intercourse. Other males were not even on my radar. Much to his displeasure, I left my job and began undertaking my nurse's training at the local university. David knew that I was much happier now that I had a concrete direction for my life. Yet David continued to feel disillusioned in his role as assistant pastor and decided he wanted to leave the church ministry. The lack of support and understanding from our senior pastor or counselor during a critical time in our lives and the leadership's continual demands of attendance at meetings while we were in crisis had become too much for him to bear. The formality of "religion" was diametrically opposed to what he truly believed. *True faith really is liberating; dead religion is not,* he thought.

One afternoon, David returned home feeling very depressed and disillusioned with his life. "I feel burnt out with being a pastor, Rachel. I am constantly busy writing newsletters and visiting people who do not really need me to visit. I don't feel like I am making any difference. I'm supposed to be a pastor and I don't even get time to read my Bible!"

As I listened to David, I knew that he needed to leave the ministry. It seemed like he was a round pin trying to fit into a square hole. David had always been interested in talking with the person on the street, the drug user or the struggling single parent. He did not do well with middle- to upper-class church people who didn't want to change.

I handed the newspaper to David, conveniently opened at the job section, smiled, and said, "There's a support worker job at a local shelter for the homeless."

"I don't know about this, Rachel. They're not going to want to take someone who has no experience." David sounded deflated.

"David, you are the perfect person for this job. You have been there yourself and you have recovered. You have managed to get a degree, settle down and get married and hold a job as a pastor for nine months. You are perfect for the job, David. Ring them now!"

I quickly grabbed the phone and handed it to David before he could change his mind. David knew that I would not shut up unless he at least tried to call.

"I guess it's worth a try. It does offer better wages, and I would be working with a cutting-edge client group with whom I am quite familiar." As the phone rang, David told me that he had imagined how it would feel to be free from the very tight restraints of the church he was working in.

He got the job! Both of us felt freed.

Alternative Lifestyles

David started working at the city shelter, which was a "crack-den" of a place. Lots of activity went on in this place, and it was very dark and seedy. The stairways were covered in vomit stains; fleas bounced all over the place; and the smells of illicit substances and alcohol were pungent in the dark and smoky corridors. The atmosphere was always charged with criminal activity, such as robberies, alcoholism, prostitution, heroin and crack cocaine use, aggression and violence. It was quite a scary place to work.

During David's time working at the shelter, I sought out another counseling agency that specialized in couple's counseling. We began to attend specialized marital counseling sessions in the downtown core of the city.

The sex therapist did not truly seem to understand the nature of vaginismus, nor did she seem to appreciate that there was a significant part of this condition that was attributed to physiological matters. She merely adopted a cognitive-behavioral approach to the problem. After researching therapy for vaginismus, it seemed there was only specialist help in America, and there were no specialists available in the UK to help with the physiological aspect of my condition. At this point, I was not even referred to or made aware of how a physiotherapist could help with pelvic floor exercises.

"David, do you have any sexual fantasies?" the young brunette counselor asked.

David, feeling a little confused and shocked at the question, wondered why the counselor would ask him such a question.

"Sorry, I don't understand what my fantasies have to do with Rachel not being able to have sex." David spoke bluntly while he glared at the counselor. I could sense that, like me, he already had a good idea of where she was heading, and like me, he was not too amused.

"Well, some clients who are struggling with sexual intimacy in their marriage choose to seek out sex from other means," the counselor continued.

"You mean to say that your advice to me in dealing with this issue is for me to seek out a prostitute?"

As I glanced over at David, I could see the look of anger on his face. I could tell by looking at him that his blood boiled. Pornography is one thing, but seeking out prostitutes is quite another thing altogether. I sat in my seat, deflated. *Is this what our marriage has come to?* I thought.

It seemed that everywhere I sought help, no one had the solution to resolving my problem. Like this counselor, they each tried to skirt around the issue and offer alternatives to addressing the main problem. As I sat quietly in my chair, tears began to fill my eyes, but I choked them back. There was no way I was going to cry in front of this woman. As I listened to her talking about introducing other partners and looking elsewhere for sex, my self-esteem plummeted that much lower. I felt like a hot mess.

As I looked toward the counselor, it seemed that like many other women, she oozed confidence and was pretty and well dressed. I left that counseling session with a new story. My story became, "I'm broken and not capable of having sex like other women. I am different and not able to be fixed, and I am wrong to expect David to remain faithful to me." Again, the counseling had not even come close to addressing our problem. Simply put, David was advised to have an emotional relationship with me, but to find sexual intimacy elsewhere. The stress between us did not go away, and even with the counseling sessions, the problem seemed to just get bigger and bigger and the suggestions more absurd and less helpful.

After the counseling had ended, I was left feeling shocked that a professional I had sought help from had suggested an open marriage idea because of my problem. As I attempted to process what had been suggested, I again was left with deep feelings of guilt for how David had become trapped in a marriage without sex and I agreed that it did seem unfair that David was being affected by my issues around having sex.

The counselor was correct in that it did not seem right that David must have his life destroyed by my problem. I began to see the logical reasons why someone would suggest the idea of an open marriage to him. At least it would mean that David could find his sexual fulfillment elsewhere.

How long do we wait until we give in? I asked myself. *When do we throw in the towel or resort to other measures in order to save our marriage? Maybe we really are kidding ourselves that our marriage can be saved. All I know right now is that I don't want to give up David, and he has made it clear that that is not what he wants either. I just want a chance to live life rather than being trapped with this problem.*

Since we had left the ministry, I felt like I had lost a lot of my faith in God and I could most definitely say I had lost a lot of my naiveté. I always looked up to the leaders of the Christian church as being perfect, thus never saw that some leaders were wolves in sheep's clothing. Since we left the church, it felt like we had been excommunicated. Everyone and everything I had ever known in life had been centered on the church.

Our phone never seemed to ring anymore, and no one ever knocked at our door. Life became very lonely, as it seemed that all of the people we knew in relation to the church were no longer interested in being acquainted with us anymore, plus our family was over an hour's drive from our house. We had tried settling into other churches in the city; however, it seemed that no matter how many churches we tried to settle in, we were unable to. As soon as people became aware of the fact that we had left the ministry, they seemed to back away.

David and I knew that we had been spiritually abused and it was going to take time to get over this. We still believed in God, but I could not honestly say that I was not still angry that He was allowing us to suffer. I sometimes wondered if God still wanted to know me. Maybe I had let Him down to such a point that He was no longer interested in me. I wanted to go home to the place I had always known as home, where my family resided, and that was sixty miles north.

We eventually moved into our own house. We hoped and believed that having a home to call our own would be the answer to our situation. However, deep down we both knew that our lack of time together and our lack of intimacy had already caused serious damage to our relationship. Vaginismus was not only slowly destroying our relationship, it was also continuing to gnaw away at both my and David's mental health.

Every day I cried, and I began to comfort eat and drink alcohol to try to numb the feelings of inadequacy I was feeling. There were days where I would just lie in my bath, staring at the hideous bright-pink walls with the tacky pink tiles with a mural of a big mermaid on it. The bathroom was not decorated the way I wanted it, since we had only recently moved into the house. Money was tight, and being new homeowners with unskilled jobs, we didn't have the time or money to decorate.

Not only were the walls and tiles pink, but the carpet was bright-pink too. I often thought that the bathroom was the opposite of what I was feeling. As I lay alone in that bathroom, I felt a strong sense of darkness come over me. I would sit for so long in the bath that I started to feel the warm water become cold against my body. But my body refused to move as I stared vacantly at the hideous pink tiles. As I lay in the cold water, I could hear David's Led Zeppelin music blaring out downstairs, which meant that he was drinking again.

As I began to think about David drinking alone in the kitchen and feeling unhappy, a strong wave of guilt engulfed me and again my eyes filled with tears. David had recovered from a life of addiction, only to become married to someone who was causing him more misery and pain. I felt the guilt of pushing him back toward the life of drinking alcohol that he had escaped.

A Nobody

As I lay in the bath, all I could think about were the words that had been said to David and me upon leaving the church ministry by the senior pastor who oversaw the pastors in our region. He had been my pastor growing up before he had been promoted to oversee pastors. He had come to visit us at our house after David had given his resignation to the church. "You're going to be a nobody. You're nothing without the ministry."

Those were the words said to us when we left the ministry by the very same pastor I had been christened by as a newborn baby. The same childhood pastor I had seen smile when Dad had made sure he had his favorite dessert at the weekly Bible study. We never heard from him again following that day, and it was as if all those childhood memories had never happened and I was just a forgotten memory. The happy memories of my childhood had been replaced with our senior pastor telling David to divorce me and then my regional superintendent pastor telling us we would be nobody. David and I were shocked; it was never meant to be this way. If only we had not experienced vaginismus, maybe we would have been effective in Christian ministry. I often wonder about what impact we could have made by serving others, but right then we were in desperate need for someone to serve us in our time of crisis.

Everyone I had looked up to and respected growing up as a child was gone from my life. I could not understand how I could have grown up in the church and then in my darkest hour, they were all gone. I truly had been left to feel like a nobody and I now questioned my very purpose in life. Growing up in the culture of Christianity and church was all I had ever known. No longer did I see anyone from the church we had pastored; it was like we were out of sight and out of mind.

I looked across at the razor sitting on the side of the bath and pondered how easy it would be just to grab the razor and end this mess. Thoughts flooded through my mind as to how I could end my life and how much better it would be if I did. I slowly picked up the razor and studied it closely. I again felt an overwhelming longing to end all the pain and torment. As I held the razor close to my wrist, shaking with fear, I wondered how it would feel—*Would it be quick?* With the razor still in my hands, I started to think about what life would be like for everyone if I did end it all. I felt trapped and in a no-win situation. If I decided to live, I would continue to feel guilty and hopeless, but if I decided to kill myself, then I would devastate my whole family and maybe even destroy their faith in God.

I knew that I desperately needed help, but where could I turn? I certainly did not like the prospect of confiding in a professional and being placed in a psychiatric ward, being pushed into taking pills to numb the devastation. I wanted an answer or a cure to my problem, not a wound dressing that would simply cover it up. But no one seemed to have even heard of vaginismus. It seemed that there was little information on the subject, and professionals used words like "Oh, you're just frigid," or "You just need to learn to relax," which did not make me feel compelled to return to their offices for help. If vaginismus was simply cured by relaxing, then one could ask the question as to why muscle relaxants, such as Ativan, and alcohol intoxication are not able to overcome vaginismus.

It certainly didn't work for me anyway, I thought.

A New Perspective

I set the razor down and got out of the tub. *I must find something that will work to overcome my vaginismus.* I had learned that I no longer wanted to live this life, and after much contemplation, I realized suicide was not the answer. In fact, it was an act that would make a sad situation even more sad and traumatic for others. My issue had caused too much devastation already, so now it was time to change my story.

I had to focus on making the change in my life that David and I so desperately needed. The time had come to slay my dragon once and for all. I had no idea how long it would take, but as I got dressed, I felt a new wave of fight rise within me. This was not how my story would end. I needed to take control of this situation since my false perceptions had led me to believe I had full control of my situation, when in reality I had been out of control most of my life. This was the beginning of my second wind, and I was determined I would win this fight, no matter how long it took.

Craving the Next Level

David worked for six months in the dangerous city shelter, then he finally got a job working for an agency that supported parents and caregivers of drug users. After a year in that job, David was accepted for the post of Substance Misuse Specialist out in a nearby rural town. After working for little money in the church, we now found ourselves blessed financially, and we were able to enjoy spending time together going to the cinema, out for meals and weekends away.

Although we still found ourselves battling the crisis with vaginismus, it never stopped us from trying to enjoy the life we had. The intensity of our crisis often came in waves and was followed by what would be described as the stages of the grieving process.

When someone grieves, they go through the stages of disbelief/shock, denial, guilt, blame and then acceptance. David and I often found that we bounced between the stages of the grieving process when it came to the loss of our sex life. Shortly thereafter, when I had completed my nurse training, David decided to undertake his psychiatric nurse training. I managed to secure a six-month temporary position in a small town near where my parents lived. Direction in our lives tightened our prospects for emigrating to Canada, something we had both often dreamed about.

It was a Saturday afternoon, and I was looking at pictures of Canada again, dreaming about what it would be like to live there. David and I missed the friends we had made there during our itinerant ministry and we often reminisced about the fun times we had and the many friends we had made. We had visited Canada together immediately after we had left Bible college and traveled to many different churches for three months, but both of us knew we had to return home for stability due to our ongoing problem.

David was listening to his music in the kitchen and cooking his usual feast. As I searched the web, I saw that there was a nursing conference nearby with visitors from all over the world. Many nurses visit these events to learn about new evidence-based practices and to meet nurse recruiters from all over the world. The event was being held in a place called Manchester, United Kingdom, which was around a sixty-minute drive from where we were living. I raced down the stairs to share with David about the conference and persuaded him that we needed to seek out jobs in Canada. As I walked into the kitchen, David stood looking out of the window, listening to Pink Floyd singing, "We don't need no education…" David turned and saw me standing there looking intently at him like I was ready to burst.

He sighed, "What now, Rachel, what have you seen? Your face is telling me that you're about to sell me an idea." I knew that was my cue to sell him my idea.

"Well, I think we should attend this nursing conference and inquire about jobs. Who knows who we will meet! This could be our chance, David! We could get offered a job and start a new life in Canada!"

"How much?" David was a Scotsman, so he was always worried about money.

"Thirty-five dollars each. I think it's worth it, David; we must go."

A few weeks later, we were at the conference talking with prospective employers from Canada. Interviews were arranged, and our dreams of moving to Canada were starting to become a reality.

"This is just what we need, David! A fresh start. We can overcome our problems and we can start again afresh. No more counselors or doctors, no more difficulties with church, just you and me."

While at the nursing conference, David and I met many different recruiters from all parts of the world. After I had stopped to look at joining the reserve forces came the moment that would change our lives for ever.

"Rachel, you're not joining the army reserve! It's too dangerous and I'm not having you go off to war when they call you up!" David often had to bring me back down to earth when my ideas became a little too extreme.

"I know, I was just looking at the training they give—it's amazing! But yes, I don't think I would do too well with the assault courses, rifle training and going to war." I placed the leaflet back and smiled at the officer and turned to walk away—and there right in front of us was a recruiter from Canada.

"David! Look!!" I screeched excitedly as I picked up my mountain of bags of free pens and gifts from the hundreds of booths that we had passed.

The recruiters were so friendly and were extremely interested in talking to us about our dreams of moving to Canada. After the recruiters shared about the need for nurses to live and work in rural towns in Northern British Columbia, David and I knew that we needed to apply. We left the conference with details for a follow-up interview for jobs in Canada and a fresh new lease on life. For a day we had dared to step out of life as we knew it and had dared to dream of a new life, and we had not spoken about our issue once that day. There was no crying or feelings of depression or loss of hope for our marriage—just thoughts of our new venture in life that we had agreed to pursue together. Now all our attention was heavily focused on preparing for interviews and researching our new prospective life in Canada.

We continued to try to seek out help for what had become a sexless marriage while we both continued to make plans to go and live in Canada. We were still able to share intimate moments together, but as the years passed by with no intervention helping, any part of becoming sexually intimate became a turn off for both of us. It had become something that did not seem enjoyable and had often ended in me crying and David feeling rejected, so avoiding all sexual intimacy had become the answer for us to survive.

We found that we could openly communicate about how we truly felt about vaginismus with each other, but we also knew that we still needed the help of a professional. I managed to contact a private gynecologist who was a rather "cold" individual who simply stated that I had vaginismus. There was a stream of other professionals that we saw while we were still residing in the United Kingdom who used comments like "frigid," and one person even stated that she "could feel a tight band up there," which planted thoughts of physiological abnormality in my mind. It seemed that there was little help available in the United Kingdom unless we sought private appointments with psychologists and psychoanalysts, which was our next move.

After leaving the church, David and I started the process of selling our house in the city and finding jobs so that we could be nearer to my family and our friends. After leaving the church we had become isolated from everyone that we had known, and we hoped that moving back nearer to family for a while would alleviate that stressor. At least we would have some distraction from our ongoing issue and would be able to experience some laughter again. The house sold quickly with good profit, and I got a job at the local hospital. The extra profit on the sale of our house allowed David to return to college to train to be a registered psychiatric nurse. David and I were happy to be returning to my hometown, but little did we know that we would not be there for too long before we would move again, and our lives would change forever.

Seed for Thought
"Fear not, for I have redeemed you; I have summoned you by name; you are mine. When you pass through the waters, I will be with you; and when you pass through the rivers, they will not sweep over you; and when you pass through the fire, you will not be burned; the flames will not set you ablaze" (Isaiah 43:1–2).

CHAPTER NINE

Dr. Frank Gets Frank

"Remember: we all get what we tolerate. So stop tolerating excuses within yourself, limiting beliefs of the past, or half-assed or fearful states."
—Tony Robbins

Do I look frigid? Do I look tense? Can people tell I am still a virgin… Paranoia, eat your heart out! I thought as I walked through the crowded shopping center, looking in the shop windows at the beautiful clothes, bags and shoes. Maybe I should try something on, just to see. I picked up a beautiful little black dress, took it to the changing room, and tried it on.

Beautiful Reminder

I stared back at my reflection in the mirror of the changing room. A beautiful young woman dressed in a cocktail dress stared back at me. I didn't see the label *frigid* or *damaged goods*; I simply saw a young woman dressed in a beautiful cocktail dress. My self-esteem was at its lowest. How could any guy ever find someone like me attractive? They might like the outward appearance, but once they began to dig beneath the superficial surface of my being, I was sure they would not like what they discovered.

Even though I continued to tell myself the daily story that other men could not find me attractive, there were many times that other men did pay attention to me. For a split second, I felt my spirits lift and a cheeky smile lit up my face. Although I struggled with achieving sexual intimacy, I still dreamed of the day that my problem would be resolved, and I would be free from the pain.

I loved watching romantic movies where the girl falls in love with the guy and then everything goes wrong, and then finally everything is made right at the end of the movie. I would cry buckets of happiness, but at the same time I would cry because I wanted the same happy ending to my story.

Since moving closer to my parents, I had gotten a job at a local hospital, and David was becoming engrossed in his studies to become trained as a nurse in mental health. He became obsessed with learning about all the different mental health disorders and was excited about learning, as he knew that he would be able to connect with people who found themselves facing a crisis. I remember while I was working a night shift as a newly qualified nurse and a young doctor decided he would dance with all the nurses. It was a strange but beautiful night. I was enjoying being back in a city where I was around my family and friends.

I enjoyed working alongside him, as he was always laughing and joking, and it seemed like he never had a care in the world. That night, he got out his headphones at 2:00 a.m. and placed one ear bud in his ear and one ear bud in my ear and said, "Listen." As I listened to the words of that song, I had to stop my eyes from tearing up. As I sat in that chair, I heard of James Blunt singing, "You're Beautiful" in the quiet office at work.

While healthcare staff laughed and completed their tasks, I sat for a few minutes and was reminded that I was beautiful. After the song had finished, he stood up and grabbed one of the older healthcare ladies and began dancing her around the office and laughing. As I sat and watched them dance, I wondered if that doctor had realized how much I needed to be reminded that others around me saw me as beautiful.

Maybe he perceived my low self-esteem and thought I needed to be reminded that I was beautiful. During my time as a nurse, I often found that I was able to connect with the patients who were challenging or who did not want to engage. On numerous occasions, patients said, "You're different from the others; it's like you understand my pain."

I had never been the alcoholic lady wheeled into emergency covered in feces after she had sat on her couch for weeks and had gotten so intoxicated, she didn't even leave the couch to go to the toilet. But something inside of me had changed, and I realized that my pain and the shame of my own disorder had taken any judgment I had about anyone I met.

Although my disorder had destroyed my confidence as a woman, men did still find me attractive. I just refused to believe it since I felt so destroyed as a woman.

Shut Down
David had reached a point where he could no longer look at me sexually. It seemed like a switch had gone off in his brain and he had shut down completely. Every day that passed was another day David had become more distant. Only our friendship held our marriage together. The hope that David once had of getting through this issue was slowly beginning to fade. He found that the counseling and behavioral techniques used to try to overcome vaginismus had made something that used to feel very natural feel very mechanical instead. Over and over in my head, I replayed the same story: *it is only a matter of time before vaginismus will destroy what is left of our intimacy.*

Sadly, we had no one apart from the professionals we were paying with whom we could openly talk about this serious issue that was destroying our marriage. Although we had confided in my mom and other members of the family, we had led them to believe that we had resolved our issues and everything was okay. Part of me felt ashamed of not being able to overcome an act that seemed so simple and natural for everyone else to achieve.

My mom never asked, and the subject was only spoken about if I raised it. I had a small number of friends but felt I could not speak with them about this condition. How could I burden my friends with such a heavy issue when professionals didn't even seem to have the answer? How could I ever bring myself to share about such an embarrassing problem as this? Vaginismus was not a problem I could simply drop into a conversation over lunch or a sociable glass of wine.

Addressing the Dragon

After much contemplation I decided that I needed to once again seek out some help. Even though all my other attempts at seeking professional help seem to have failed, I couldn't give up. I picked up the local telephone directory as I flopped down onto the sofa and stuck my feet up on the coffee table. All morning I'd been thinking about how I could get to the root problem of what was wrong with me. Maybe a psychiatrist could unearth some memory that I had repressed deep in my unconscious mind? I picked up the phone, nervously dialed the number and was put through to the voicemail of a psychiatrist named Frank. His voice sounded friendly, caring and calm. Suddenly, I found myself not knowing what to say, so I quickly hung up the phone.

The seriousness of my situation began to play in my mind. I was in my early twenties and trying to contact a psychiatrist! I'd always believed that psychiatrists were for people who were seriously messed up or for people who could not cope.

Do I really need the help of a psychiatrist? I thought. *Would he diagnose me as being mentally ill or try to pump me full of drugs?*

A few minutes later the phone rang and when I answered, I heard a friendly, soft and calming voice. "Hello, my name is Frank. Was someone from this phone trying to reach me?"

Hypnotized by his friendly and soothing voice, I openly shared my story through tears. "Do you think you could help me?"

"I can help you," Frank replied. "Do you want to come and see me this Thursday at 5:00 p.m.? The cost will be sixty-eight dollars for a fifty-minute session." Frank continued to gently assure me that he could help me, and I found myself believing that I had finally found someone who could help us.

Frank's office was in a beautiful old English house, and as we walked up the old wooden creaky stairs to his office, I began to feel my stomach somersault. David had agreed to attend the first session with me, as he knew that I was nervous about seeing a psychiatrist.

A slim, gray-haired, tanned man greeted us with a big smile.

"Come in, Rachel, and sit down. I am guessing this is David." Frank turned to David and shook his hand. As we made ourselves comfortable, Frank returned to his seat behind his big wooden desk and opened a new file folder. I sat, nervous and vulnerable, wondering what Frank was going to unearth from inside of me. Frank sat relaxed behind his desk with a questionnaire that he went through, asking about my childhood and family.

I answered his questions, and Frank told us that while I was clearly anxious and angry about my situation, he did not perceive any mental health issues in his initial assessment that required further intervention. Frank sat back in his big leather chair while he observed my tense body language.

"You look so tense, Rachel. I don't think you even know how or what a true state of relaxation feels like." Frank was right. I truly did not know what it felt like to feel relaxed. I had always felt tense.

"I would like to do some deep relaxation therapy with you, Rachel. I think this will benefit you a great deal if we can manage to get you to relax."

"I don't want to be hypnotized! My beliefs don't allow me to be hypnotized!" I had always been taught that allowing someone to take control of your thoughts or to free your mind of whatever you were thinking about leaves a person open to becoming controlled by evil spirits. Even yoga sessions had been deemed dangerous, so Frank's request for me to lose complete control under the spell of his voice was something I felt that I should not do.

As Frank listened to what he perceived as religious nonsense freely spill out of my mouth, he became angry at the damage he perceived the church had caused. "If you don't learn to relax, Rachel, then you are in danger of enduring serious effects on your health in later life. If you don't learn to relax, you will be screwed up by the time you're forty," Frank said with a serious tone. He perceived that I carried a lot of guilt and shame in relation to my disorder. He knew that being raised in a religious family could often cause an individual to feel that sex was wrong due to the extreme pressure placed on believers to remain celibate until marriage.

As Frank continued to delve into my childhood and beliefs, I began to question what I had been taught about sex before marriage. I had been taught that engaging in a sexual relationship was wrong and sinful until a person gets married. Then suddenly, literally overnight, I was expected to retrain my mind to accept that what was always unacceptable and sinful was now what was expected and natural.

Research has indicated that "strict religious upbringing, negative sexual experiences, and a lack of sexual education are the leading contributing factors for vaginismus."[6] However, it would be unfair to claim that every woman brought up in a religious home will be subject to vaginismus. Women are certainly more at risk of developing vaginismus if the religious beliefs in the home are sexually negative. For example, Frank shared with me that if a woman has learned to believe that sex is wrong and sinful, rather than being advised that sex is a wonderful gift that should be saved for the one you love, then the woman may be at risk of attaching negative beliefs to sex.

I was to learn later from another doctor, who specialized in treating vaginismus, that many of the patients he has treated have not been exposed to these particular church life experiences. There are women who have vaginismus due to an unknown cause, reinforcing the theory that every woman's case of vaginismus is unique. Stereotyping every woman into one of these categories is not the answer to curing vaginismus. Each woman travels on a unique journey and has her own reason for experiencing vaginismus.

While growing up, I had attended church with my family and had listened to many sermons about sexual infidelity. With Frank's help, I continued to reflect on what I'd been taught. I remembered one incident that occurred at church where I had watched a young, pregnant woman, who was unmarried, be publicly humiliated in front of the whole church. I had witnessed the sheer disgust and disappointment from the leaders she had been taught to respect as they learned of the young woman's shame.

Suppressed

As I continued to search my childhood for answers, I soon realized that it was not surprising that I was having difficulty with sex. In my world, sex was only talked about in a negative way or avoided altogether. Contraception was also not a subject that was openly discussed when I was a teenager, as it was not deemed necessary for me to know

---

6 Yosra Zgueb, Uta Ouali, Radhouane Achour, Rabaa Jomli and Fethi Nacef, "Cultural aspects of vaginismus therapy: a case series of Arab-Muslim patients," *the Cognitive Behaviour Therapist,* Volume 12 (January 2019) https://www.cambridge.org/core/journals/the-cognitive-behaviour-therapist/article/cultural-aspects-of-vaginismus-therapy-a-case-series-of-arabmuslim-patients/EB14A87F556D7D4B82D76A1BA8013C96/core-reader.

about it since I was not sexually active. My parents were strict Christians, and they had been taught that it was their duty to ensure that I kept myself pure.

There had been heavy pressure from my church and family to remain celibate. Mom would quiz me after I had been out alone with guys. Even six months or more into my relationship with David, Mom kept visiting me with cups of tea and cake if I were alone in my bedroom with David for too long, and she had a look of fear and concern on her face.

Looking back, I began to realize that there were a lot of questions regarding sex that I had not had answered. I had been totally unprepared for my wedding night. For someone who has been raised in a religious environment, the wedding night is perceived as an especially important event. When people cohabit for years or have one-night stands, they do not experience the pressure that a couple experiences when they are expected to perform when everybody suddenly decides that it is acceptable to perform. I remembered thinking on my wedding night that everyone would know that I was having sex, an act I had previously been taught was wrong and dirty if performed before marriage.

As I sat in Frank's office, I also remembered the pressure of having to consummate my marriage for it to be deemed legally binding. When people have premarital sex, it is often unplanned and the whole family and church are unaware that a person is engaging in sex. If a person decides that they are not ready to have sex, it is not such a big deal. I had reached out to Frank to help find the root cause for the vaginismus. I had begun to think that I may have been molested and had maybe blocked it out somehow. However, it had never occurred to me that my strict religious upbringing could have contributed to my suffering with this disorder.

Story Stacking
After years of wondering why I had struggled so much with intimacy and sex, it was suddenly all starting to make sense and it was as if some of the guilt and the shame I had been carrying for so long had been lifted, like a heavy weight being lifted from someone's back. I was still responsible for resolving my issues, but I started to realize that having this disorder was not my fault. It was simply the messages and the stories

about sex that I had collected over the years that had caused me to become afflicted with such a disorder. I was thankful that Frank had been professional enough to call me back that day. He had given me hope for the future.

As I continued my session with Frank, I began to talk about my Christian faith and how I had always relied on God in times of trouble. "Over and over again, I have cried out to God who is supposed to love me, begging Him to take this problem away. I just don't understand… and I feel so angry—angry toward God for giving me this twisted and cruel disorder."

"I don't think that your God would want you to suffer this way either, Rachel. The beliefs that you have been taught surrounding sex are what have contributed to you suffering with this disorder. You received barely any sexual education to prepare you for your wedding night. It's not your fault. You have grown up in a world where suppressing sexual desires is deemed normal behavior and, yes, it has messed you up," Frank said.

Frank was right. But why did I have vaginismus and not every other woman in the church? There were many women in our church who had been raised in the same religious upbringing, and they didn't have a problem. Although I agree that suppressing sexual desires is not healthy, the Bible is clear on its stance of engaging in sex before marriage. However, suppressing sexuality to a point that it is never talked or joked about or discussed as an enjoyable act is harmful as it can lead to perceiving sex as a shameful act.

"It just doesn't seem fair that I am the one who has been afflicted with not being able to have sex, when I have faithfully remained pure. I'm so angry and I feel so bitter. I have never experienced anger like this before; it's like my body is vibrating with anger right now."

As I spoke about my anger, I almost felt a sense of release, like the anger that had been repressed for years now had permission to rage. "I used to feel sorry for teenage girls who had been left alone to raise a baby. Now I look at them and I just feel so much anger. It should be them who are punished, not me! Why is this happening to me?"

Once the session had come to an end, I was emotionally and physically exhausted. The session had not involved David this time and he only remained present during the session for support. He sat quietly and listened. Frank stood up and walked over to the office door. "You will get through this, Rachel. I have no idea how long your recovery is going to take, but you will overcome this."

As I continued to see Frank over the next months, we addressed a lot of the emotional problems I had experienced from suffering with vaginismus. However, it did not seem to be solving the physical issue I still experienced—the extreme pain and the involuntary spasm of the muscles in my vagina. Again, we had spent a great deal of money on professional help that seemed to be getting us nowhere. We found that we were spending the small amount of money we had left over each month on counseling sessions, which left us no money for fun or vacation. When progress halted, I stopped seeing Frank. However, I will be forever grateful to Frank, who allowed me to clearly see some of the reasons as to why my vaginismus occurred.

Purpose in Life
For many years I asked myself the question that had haunted my every waking thought: *What is my purpose in life?*

If I could not have children or completely fulfill my role as a wife, then what was my purpose? I began to wonder if my whole life was merely centered on attending work every day and nothing else. I craved so much more from life than this. I wanted to be the good wife who made my husband happy and I wanted to have a family of my own and be a great mom.

I longed to have deeper friendships, but instead I found that my friendships remained very superficial. I did not want to risk anyone finding out that I was messed up. I found that my purpose of wanting to be engaged in Christian ministry, ministering to others who were struggling, seemed to remain on a very long pause button. I wondered how long God would keep me in this place of waiting. Waiting for a family, waiting to become a mom, waiting to overcome my sexual disorder, and waiting to get my life back on track. Purpose means a lot to me, and life just seemed meaningless without purpose.

Loss and Grief

Week after week and year after year, I continued to bounce from sex therapists to psychiatrists to doctors and counselors, none of whom seemed to have the skill or expertise to release me from this ongoing nightmare of vaginismus. David and I found ourselves growing further and further apart. David rarely came near me; we didn't kiss or hold hands. I dressed up sexually, but neither David nor I saw a sexually appealing woman anymore.

Many women with vaginismus find that the condition not only affects their sex lives, but also seeps into many other areas of their lives. Simply having a conversation with colleagues at work can turn into an anxiety-provoking episode. For example, many women find themselves suddenly excluded from conversations when other women are bonding while sharing stories about their children or pregnancies.

Vaginismus is a serious condition that potentially leaves many women without the prospect of ever having children. Some women have managed to have a child through other means, such as artificial insemination or adoption. However, for a variety of reasons, other women find themselves childless.

Even going to celebrations can be upsetting. Many women with vaginismus find it traumatic to attend baby showers, christenings or dedication services, since this reinforces their feelings of loss. Women with vaginismus often avoid sitting with groups of women, since they know that they will eventually be asked the questions they always dread.

These include, "Do you have children?" "When are you going to have a baby?" or "Time's ticking away, girlfriend—better get on it quick!"

Such comments and questions can result in women suffering a complete meltdown and reverting to a state of depression. Merely seeing a pregnant woman in the street can cause the woman with vaginismus and her partner to experience the sense of grief and loss all over again.

Freedom behind Bars

After my nurse's training, I found a job working with young male prisoners. It was no easy job, but I loved every minute I got to spend behind bars. Strangely enough, it was not until I began to work behind bars that

I was set free from a lot of insecurities in my own life. I had been very shy and unsure of myself on entering the prison environment; however, this was quickly knocked out of me! I found myself working in quite a different environment from what I was used to; however, it turned out to be the one place in my life where I truly felt that I belonged.

I grew in confidence, lost around thirty-five pounds of weight, and felt amazing. I was making a difference in people's lives and was accepted for just being who I was. Vaginismus had affected every part of my life and it had made me feel worthless. If there was a time in my life that I had felt strong enough to confide in someone about my vaginismus, it was then.

David and I found the denial phase lifting and once again felt that we were strong enough to try to face our problem again. We had moved closer to family, we had gained employment as nurses that we were happy with, but we wanted children.

Brothers, friends and cousins were all creating their own little families, but we remained unable to have children of our own. We decided to try cognitive behavioral therapy with a psychologist. This psychologist was a highly skilled professional who saw people all over the UK for therapy. His sessions cost $165 US for a fifty-minute session, and every week David and I drove one hundred miles to meet with our psychologist.

After our first session with the psychologist, I knew he was highly skilled and could help me. He both understood how I was feeling and gave David and me practical homework that attacked our negative thoughts surrounding sex.

The combination of cognitive behavioral therapy and working in the prison environment helped me remove a lot of my negative thinking, poor self-esteem and suicidal thoughts. I learned the art of changing my thoughts, which then changed my feelings, which then changed my behavior.

While I worked behind bars, I had a lot of my judgmental thoughts and beliefs challenged. Not everything in life was black and white like I had been taught. Sometimes life isn't straightforward and gray areas occur, which often don't fit into society's norms. Like me, there are many people living in the gray areas who are, in fact, wonderful people but who have been labeled as sinners and who even to this day are sadly often ostracized from attending church.

While I worked in the prison environment, it became a place where I began to have my beliefs and values challenged and a place where I found freedom. I questioned everything I had been taught over and over and realized that a lot of what I had been taught in church had been wrong. I still held onto my faith but stomped the religion out of my life.

The cognitive behavioral treatment did not completely resolve my vaginismus, but it did help to resolve a lot of the surrounding issues. It significantly helped with the emotional aspects of vaginismus, but I still struggled with finding a solution to the physical component of the disorder. I had come to the point where I had learned to accept that what was happening to me was not my fault. Even though I could not have sex, I was still a woman and a wife. I would never give up hope of finding a cure and after all my perseverance, it seemed that I might have finally found a cure. This was the last professional that we saw before we left the UK to go and live in Canada. Like I said, we were soon to leave my hometown once again, but this time it was for good.

Seed for Thought

"The purposes of a man's heart are deep waters, but a man of understanding draws them out" (Proverbs 20:5).

CHAPTER TEN

North American Victories

"Power is not given to you. You have to take it."
—*Beyoncé Knowles Carter*

I quickly dropped off my radio and keys at the prison reception and frantically rushed out the front door.

"Where's the fire, Rachel?" an officer shouted from the station. I tried to get through the door with my hands loaded with bags and turned back to look at the officer.

"There's no fire, Sam. Of all the days that I desperately need to get home, my car is in the garage getting serviced. Anyway, I have to rush. Bye, Sam." I made my way down the steep hill toward home, only thinking about my phone interview for a nursing position in Canada.

In one hour, they would be phoning me.

David had already completed his interview for the position of a community mental health nurse and had been offered a full-time job, so the heat was on for me to pass my interview.

After almost reaching the bottom of the hill, I saw what looked like David's car heading toward me. Screeching to an abrupt halt on the side road that I was about to cross, David rolled down the window and shouted to me to jump in.

"I thought you were at work today," I said.

"I got off early so that I could get you home in time for your interview."

A few minutes after we arrived, the phone began to ring. I nervously picked up the phone. "Hello?"

With that hello, our journey to Canada began.

A New Life

After a whirlwind of filling out paperwork, dealing with immigration and selling our house, we found ourselves in Manchester Airport waiting to board a one-way flight to Canada. This was to be the start of a new life for us—not just professionally, but personally, as well.

Twenty-four hours later we arrived at a small rural oil and gas town of only twelve thousand people where we would live for the next three years—a small town located in British Columbia, Canada. Now living in the middle of nowhere with no distractions, we knew we must turn our attention once more to our sexless marriage. Vaginismus had taken over our lives, and both David and I needed to be in a place where we would have no distractions. As soon as we got off the small plane and saw the airport, we knew that life was going to be quite different. There were no cafes or shops, and the airport was the size of one airport gate. We only had to wait minutes for our baggage, rather than hours like we did in the UK. When we stepped outside the airport, all we could see was a big open road and endless fields and trees. Apart from a few food shops, diners and work, there was little else to do and the neighboring towns were at least a one to two-hour drive. David had been given a full-time job working in community mental health and addictions, and I had a full-time job working with psychiatry inpatients for two years and then moved to emergency nursing.

Canada was our time for a fresh start and a time for both of us to explore who we were without any external expectations to meet. Going on a journey of self-exploration is not an easy task and on some occasions my search for my identity became so painful that addiction became something that befriended me. I never understood how addiction could take over a person's life until I found myself going from one to two glasses of wine every night.

I sometimes look at my life and wonder how I never ended up dead or in a seclusion room. Life truly does look different in times of pain and suffering. Life truly is precious, and it can change so quickly for the better or for the worse. How can we ever know that at some point in our lifetime we are not going to become the homeless bag lady or the alcoholic guy we see sitting on that bench in the park? No one goes into marriage thinking that everything is going to go wrong—that they are going to get divorced, have an affair or go through losing a child. We do not know what the next hour of our life will bring, which is why people say that every day should be lived as if it were your last day on earth.

One evening I sat as usual in the basement of our new house, surfing the internet. There was not much else to do, as it was forty below zero outside and David was asleep in front of the TV. I could only visit Wal-Mart so many times, so the winter months became exceptionally long and lonely.

As I had done many times before, I typed "vaginismus" into the Google search to see if there was some miraculous cure for my issue that I might have missed before. I'd imagined myself with two children as we sat with our family opening presents on Christmas morning; however, it was merely a fantasy. Instead, I sat alone in my basement desperately searching for answers that did not seem to exist.

After searching the internet for a while, I decided to type the word "vaginismus" into YouTube. I was tired of being alone with this disorder and found myself desperately wanting to connect with someone else who was struggling with vaginismus. So many professionals had told me that there were many women like me who were unable to have sex, but I had never seen them. I needed to be reassured that these other women existed.

As the YouTube video popped up, I saw a middle-aged lady talking about her experience with vaginismus. As I listened to the attractive lady talk about her experience, I felt relieved that I had seen another woman who was struggling with vaginismus. I was not alone.

Hope with Botox

The woman claimed that she had been cured with Botox treatment! I quickly typed the doctor's name into the YouTube tab. As I began to watch the videos that the specialist had posted, I started to cry again, but this time I felt a glimmer of hope. I researched the procedure and emailed the doctor's office for further details. I did not relish the thought of having Botox injected into my vagina, but this might just work!

A few days later, I received an email back from the doctor and after reading the email, I decided to call David down to the basement to see the doctor's video. David gave a large frustrated sigh when I eagerly shared with him about the video, but after a few minutes of watching the video, David found himself beginning to agree with me that this might possibly be the answer we had been searching for.

"You have to book it, Rachel; we need to do this!" It seemed that David had felt the same glimmer of hope that I had experienced when I first watched the doctor's video.

We scheduled a date for the procedure and booked our flights from Seattle to New York. We had decided that we were going to make this whole experience as positive as we possibly could.

Driving down the open road toward the town of Jasper in Alberta, Canada, I rolled down the windows of the truck and blasted Lady Gaga. "I can't believe that we are actually doing this, David. If people knew that we were traveling so far to meet a doctor that we have never met and to have him inject Botox into my vagina, they would surely say that I was crazy."

"Well, I think it is good, Rachel. I think this is going to work, I really do," David said reassuringly.

"I hope so, David, because if this doesn't work, then I don't think there are any more options available to us."

David placed his hand on my knee. "It's going to work, Rachel. I just know it's going to work."

After a five-hour journey, we arrived at Jasper to meet our good friends Molly and Hugh. I stood in awe of the beautiful Canadian Rockies every time I visited Jasper.

After a few days of hikes, eating, and fun in Jasper, we hit the road to Seattle. Our next stop would be New York, a city we had never experienced before. After arriving in New York City, we spent a few days in Times Square, then took the train from Penn Station to Boston on Sunday, David's birthday. All these activities provided me with great distraction therapy from the upcoming treatment. There was so much to do day and night, so anytime I began to feel myself becoming anxious,

I would crowd my mind with the many activities of New York. After arriving in Boston, we boarded the bus to Manchester, New Hampshire.

We were now only one hour away from the place that we hoped would provide us with the cure to my vaginismus. Tomorrow I would place myself in the doctor's care. There was no turning back.

Slaying My Dragon
"Come on, babe, it's six a.m. and you need to be getting ready," David said as he sat smiling on the side of the bed, bright-eyed and ready for the day to start. I was hopeful but nervous, and nerves and negative thoughts started to take control of my mind as I walked to the bathroom to get showered. Panic rose from the pit of my stomach, and a sudden wave of a nausea swept over me. I had read a lot of information about Botox and its side effects and how some people had even died from having Botox.

As I continued to get ready, I battled against the crazy thoughts that were running through my head. *You're going to put Botox into your vagina when many people still question the safety of placing it into the face to remove wrinkles!* As a nurse I had thoroughly researched Botox, and logically I knew that under the circumstances it was quite reasonable to be placing Botox into my vaginal muscles to relax them, but it still didn't stop irrational thoughts flooding my mind.

When we arrived at the doctor's office, a nurse greeted us and escorted us to the waiting room. An anesthesiologist went through my history and patiently explained everything that was about to happen. I soon met the doctor who was going to perform the procedure that I hoped would change my life. He had a big, genuine smile and took his time explaining the procedure.

The Botox would be injected into the areas of my vagina so that he could identify which muscles were involuntarily contracting in order to paralyze them. Once the muscles had been identified and paralyzed, we could then begin to retrain them with dilators. After being reassured, I was taken to the preoperative room and placed in a gown. While I lay nervously in bed with David by my side, the anesthesiologist placed an IV into my hand and started a bag of fluid to hydrate me. He then administered one milligram of Versed (intravenous valium) to help me relax.

I was then taken into the operating room, where the doctor slowly and very patiently did an internal examination. I could hear and see the doctor and was aware of what he was doing but felt relaxed from the Versed. He began with a Q-tip to test for pain involving the vulva and then inserted a finger to see which muscles contracted. As David stood by my side holding my hand for support, I slowly felt myself losing contact with reality. The sound of my heart beating on the cardiac monitor became more distant as I felt myself drifting into a deep sleep.

"See you later; you are going to feel sleepy now, Rachel," the doctor said. That was the last thing I remember about the procedure. I felt no pain and was totally unaware of what was taking place during the procedure.

David told me later that, as he stood by the doctor's side, he began to see me struggle and clench my thighs. The doctor explained that I was completely unaware of what was happening and was fully sedated. As David watched my involuntary movements, he suddenly realized that my problem was not only psychological but physiological too. David watched as the doctor inserted the Botox and did a more in-depth and detailed examination of my vagina.

"She is completely normal, David; her anatomy is perfect," the doctor said reassuringly.

"So, when Rachel was lifting her buttocks and clenching her thighs, she was completely unconscious?" David asked. He couldn't believe that someone's body could still fight even when they were unaware of what was happening.

"That's correct, David. Rachel would not have been able to feel the procedure taking place. She was sedated heavily with Propofol, so she was unaware of what was taking place." David had always believed that my extreme physical reaction to him attempting sex was in some way me rejecting him. He could now clearly see that he was wrong. For eleven years, I had genuinely not been able to have sex. My body truly had been saying no.

As I emerged from deep sleep, I saw David at my bedside, holding my hand and smiling. "Is it done yet?" I was still groggy from the anesthetic. David began to explain to me what he had seen, but I was still full of anesthesia, too busy laughing and talking nonsense. David smiled as he watched his wife being wheeled into the recovery room giggling to herself. "I feel stoned, David."

When I eventually awoke, the recovery nurse informed me that everything had gone very well and in fact, I had the biggest dilator in place.

"The biggest dilator is in me right now?" I asked.

"Take a look, Rachel," David said. "I saw the doctor put it in while you were under the sedation and you dilated in around thirty seconds."

As I sat and listened to David, I was shocked that I could not feel the dilator.

How could something that had caused so much pain be inside of me now and not be causing any pain? I pulled up the blankets and felt between my legs. Sure enough, I felt the end of the biggest blue dilator at the entrance of my vagina. "The whole dilator is completely inside of me!"

The recovery nurse explained that the dilator was coated with lidocaine and the doctor had injected some local anesthetic into the walls of my vagina along with the Botox.

Road to Recovery

As I recovered from the procedure, a wonderful nurse looked after me, monitoring my blood pressure and pulse and assisting with changing and moving the dilators. Even when I changed the dilator for a smaller one, I still found that I experienced no pain! After eleven years of battling vaginismus, I had almost given up hope that I would ever be able to have something inside of my vagina without experiencing excruciating pain.

As I turned toward David, I saw relief and happiness in his face. At last, there had been a breakthrough, and I knew that the long journey to New Hampshire and the financial debt had this time been worth it.

David informed me that as the doctor inserted the injections and carried out the internal examination, I had begun to arch my back and tense my thighs, despite being under anesthesia. The doctor had explained that this in itself was evidence that people who suffer with vaginismus truly have no control over that spasm. Even unconsciously, my body was still causing the vagina to spasm. Thus, telling someone to just try to relax is not going to change anything.

All through the years I had questioned the diagnosis, wondering if the doctors were missing something crucial. They had been. I had also been given a lot of wrong information from professionals about there being a tight band that they could feel and one doctor suggesting I was frigid. When the doctor visited me in the recovery room and explained that I had a completely normal vagina of normal length and size, I cried tears of joy that someone had finally taken the time to look and reassure me that there were no underlying problems.

After I was fully awake and alert, I was given some food and drink and then I could be discharged back to the hotel with David to sleep off the anesthesia. However, I was in no way feeling overly tired and I very much wanted to see the sights and resume our vacation.

The doctor directed us to see his secretary for some maps so that we could go to the mountains in New Hampshire. The journey was somewhat interesting, as I had the purple dilator inside of me, which had to remain in for around thirty-six hours. I sat awkwardly on a doughnut-shaped cushion. When I got out of the car in Portland, Maine, I resembled a pregnant woman with a bad back, waddling along with her legs apart!

As we walked around the shops, we laughed at some of the comments that passersby must have been making. I knew that I must have looked strange, but I didn't care. I was simply happy that I was finally on the road to recovering from this hellish nightmare. The longer I walked around with the dilator inside of me, the more comfortable it seemed to become. If I made a sudden movement, I would find myself wincing from a pain that felt like someone pinching me, but it was nothing compared with the pain I had experienced living with vaginismus.

Taking Back Control

After we finished dinner at a restaurant, I anxiously went back to the washroom and attempted to reinsert the dilator, which had slipped while we were eating. I hoped that it wouldn't take me an hour to put it back in! After coating the dilator with generous amounts of lidocaine, I took a deep breath and attempted to push it back into place. As I pushed the dilator against the entrance of my vagina, I could feel it slide right back into place! There was no burning, no knife-like pain and no resistance!

Within fewer than ten seconds the dilator had slid with ease back into my vagina. For the first time ever, I allowed myself to believe that I had been cured.

David waited at the table. I grinned from ear to ear. "It's back in, David, and it didn't hurt one bit." As David got up from the table, he grabbed hold of my hand.

"See, I told you that it would work. I just knew that this was going to work."

That evening, I slept with the dilator in place all night. The dilators were flexible and soft and a lot more comfortable than the hard-plastic dilators I had been given up until this point. The next day, I awoke with what felt like a new lease on life, and there were no negative thoughts in my head. I felt more positive than I had felt in years. I could see by David's face and his body language that he too was starting to feel a sense of hope.

We returned to the doctor's office in the morning and went to an assigned bed to begin dilating with the bigger dilator, nicknamed "Mrs. Pink." There were two other women in the room who had also received the Botox treatment. The doctor's nurse gave a talk and allowed the women to talk with one another about their experiences while they sat or lay dilating.

Each woman had her own bed with a curtain for privacy so that she was able to dilate alone. I felt so comforted by the fact that I had now physically met other women who were also suffering with vaginismus. I was not a freak—and neither were they! Every time I had to take a dilator out and change to another size, I could feel my mind starting to work on overdrive, worried that it was going to hurt. But each time I inserted and reinserted a dilator, I felt no pain, resistance or discomfort. The pain had truly disappeared. I was filled with joy that I had finally overcome my vaginismus.

As we sat in the counseling and education classes together, we shared our experiences and fears, which felt very empowering. Many women struggled with the same problem, evidenced by the other women in the room beside me. David was able to ask questions and share his experiences of his struggles of living with a woman who was struggling with vaginismus.

The doctor explained that we might begin to experience some feelings of apprehension about continuing our treatment alone. He explained that even though I had been physically cured, it was still going to take time and effort to completely overcome vaginismus. It was now time to continue our treatment and transition to having sexual intercourse.

"Rachel, now that you have had this treatment and you have been able to successfully get a dilator inside of you, can you now picture yourself being able to have sexual intercourse with David?" the doctor asked.

"Yes, but I picture it as being awkward the first few times," I replied.

"That's okay. The difference is that you are now able to see a future of having sex, whereas before the treatment you were not even able to dream of this happening," the doctor said, smiling.

It was now time to go home and begin working toward a new life of intimacy together.

Seed for Thought
"But he said to me, 'My grace is sufficient for you, for my power is made perfect in weakness.' Therefore I will boast all the more gladly about my weaknesses, so that Christ's power may rest on me. That is why, for Christ's sake, I delight in weaknesses, in insults, in hardships, in persecutions, in difficulties. For when I am weak, I am strong" (Second Corinthians 12:9–10).

CHAPTER ELEVEN

Hopes and Dreams

"Intimacy is not purely physical; it is the act of connecting with someone so deeply, you feel like you can see into their soul." —Author unknown

Once we arrived home, we were strict with moving forward with the dilation treatment. As the days went on, I began to feel like dilating had become part of my daily routine. One day, while I was in the bathroom doing my dilation treatment, I began to think that overcoming vaginismus was just like having any other disorder. For example, when someone is a diabetic, they must accept it and plan their life around coping with their diabetes. Every day they must prick their finger and check their sugar level and adjust their medication accordingly. Sometimes they will have times when their blood sugar is too high or too low through no fault of their own, but they must adjust their routine, diet and medication in order to become balanced again.

When someone has vaginismus, she too perceives the problem, and once the spasm has been broken by the Botox, she is able to retrain the muscles and then better manage and cope with the disorder using dilators.

After just over a week had passed since receiving the Botox, I had begun to feel more comfortable with inserting the dilators and I felt more ready than I had ever felt to attempt sexual intercourse. It was a Saturday afternoon, and David and I had been watching a National Geographic program.

Breaking Through!
"I think I might be ready, David." I stood in the hallway dressed in a silky black nightgown. I had managed to dilate up to the biggest blue dilator with ease, so I knew that it was now or never. David followed me to the bedroom, and after a few minutes David was able to put the tip of his penis in with no pain whatsoever.

"Are you sure it's in there?" I did not feel any pain.

"Yep, it's in there, should I slide it in further?"

"No, let's just leave it at that today. It has been positive, and I don't want to push things too soon," I replied.

A few days later, again, we took it slow, and I used the blue dilator prior to attempting intercourse. With lots and lots of K-Y Jelly, we succeeded! This time, David managed to get all the way in! No spasm and it no longer hurt!

It felt so nice, a feeling that I could never have dreamed possible. Every time I had thought of having sex, I'd always automatically associated it with extreme pain and burning, which often left me feeling nauseated. Now I had David inside of me and it felt wonderful. My hellish nightmare had finally come to an end.

David was fully inside of me, and I was starting to cry with tears of happiness.

"Rachel, are you okay? Am I hurting you? Do you want me to stop?" David said with a confused look on his face.

"No, I just never thought I would see this day, David. I never thought I would be capable of having sex. I just can't believe it doesn't hurt anymore."

I finally felt like a normal woman. I felt like the doctor had given me my life back and a weight of guilt and shame had just suddenly been lifted from me. David didn't go any further that day. We decided to take everything slowly and we spent some time just lying together on our bed, holding each other. It felt wonderful to know that I no longer needed to keep preparing for the next step. I could relax and enjoy kissing and being intimate without worrying that it would all go wrong. A few days later David was able to move inside of me, and it remained pain free. Our sex life still had to be planned as I would need to start dilating an hour before sex, which meant that we still did not have any spontaneity, but at least we were able to have sex. Our sex life was still somewhat mechanical as I still had to take analgesia, place dilators and keep them in right up until the point that David was ready to have intercourse.

It was difficult at times, as the dilators would slip out. After being so long without sex, it was a long process to switch from exercises in the bedroom to sexual intimacy in the bedroom. David found that he began to have some difficulty getting an erection, as there had been so many difficulties with having sex for so long that he struggled to make the switch.

David was still over the moon about the breakthrough, and the next day when he went to work his coworkers saw that his face was beaming. I worked in the department next door to David and when I visited his unit to pick up some medication, he gave me the biggest smile and held my eyes with his. It was a look that I had not witnessed in many years.

Feeling Normal

The next day, while I ate lunch with colleagues, for the first time ever I was able to involve myself in a discussion about having children without feeling upset. I could now see myself having a chance like any other woman at becoming pregnant someday.

That feeling of being alone and isolated had now gone and this feeling itself was worth having the Botox treatment. As we continued to work on having sex, I began to feel a sense of normalcy that I had not experienced before. I no longer felt like the freak that I had felt like before. I'd overcome something that had been allowed to torture me for over eleven years.

After finally succeeding with sexual intercourse, I ran with pride and joy to my computer to email the doctor to inform him of our good news. I also told him that after things settled I would very much like to be an advocate and help in any way that I could with bringing vaginismus to light. I did not know how I could best help, but if there were anything I could do, I would be most willing.

I thought about a change in career direction, maybe even taking a counseling or trauma course to better help other people, and sharing my story with others. I still felt fragile with being open, but after I had beaten this and healed, I wanted to educate people and support people through this horrible ordeal.

It seemed that the violent storm that had plagued us for eleven years had finally come to an end. The tornado had now gone, but we now had to mend the damage it had left behind. The physical component of vaginismus had been cured, but all the damage to our intimacy as a couple needed to be mended. All the emotional hurt it had caused and the destruction it had done to our mental health and social and family relationships had to be addressed. However, destruction can sometimes lead to the beginning of something more wonderful.

A Family

As the sound of "You're Beautiful" by James Blunt echoed throughout the bedroom, I contentedly rested in David's arms. As I turned and passionately kissed David, I felt a wave of sexual excitement that I had only just begun to experience. I was one million miles away from the Rachel I had once been. Now, when we kissed, I felt myself becoming excited and had no desire to stop.

As David continued to caress my body, I felt myself slowly beginning to lose control in a positive way, but this time, I felt no fear. Sex was no longer painful, and for the first time in my life, I relaxed. Happiness could exist for us.

"Wow! That felt amazing!" David said, as he sat himself up in bed.

"It still feels like we are living a dream," I said. "I guess this is what the honeymoon phase would have felt like. Hey, you know that we can now classify ourselves as 'normal' then?" I was free now, free from the claws of vaginismus that had controlled my life for eleven years.

"Do you think we would make good parents, David?" I asked, while pouring the remainder of the red wine that was sitting on our bedroom dresser for the two of us.

"I think we would make great parents! Do you think we would make good parents?" David asked.

"I think so!" I had always hoped that I would become a mom one day. However, until now, I had never even dared to believe that it might actually happen. "I don't think we would have made good parents while we were suffering with vaginismus, but yeah, I do think now that we're okay, it's maybe time that we started to consider starting a family of our own."

Beaming from ear to ear, David jumped up and moved closer to me and grabbed hold of my hands.

"Are you serious about this, Rachel? 'Cause there is nothing that I would want more than to have a baby to call our own."

"I am serious, David. I think we have lost enough time from the vaginismus and I think the sooner we start trying, the better. It's funny because I have never been able to picture myself being a mom, but now I can."

The Corset

As the months of my recovery rolled by, my confidence grew, and I began to rediscover myself as a woman. I was so happy that I was finally able to demonstrate to David that I loved him. Sex began to feel freer and more exciting.

One afternoon after cooking the supper, I quickly ran up to the bedroom and pulled out the brand-new corset I had purchased that week while out shopping alone. After putting on the black stockings, panties and high-heeled shoes, I pulled the corset up over my hips and stomach and began to tighten the hooks on the back. As I neared halfway, I suddenly realized that I could not reach any further up.

"How is a person meant to put this on as a surprise?" I stared at my own reflection in the mirror. Suddenly, I had the bright idea to turn the corset around to my front so that I could continue. However, I soon realized that once I got it fastened to the top, I could not turn it back around again. Suddenly, the front door opened, and I realized that I had run out of time!

"Hey, Rachel, it's only me!" David shouted, as he took off his shoes and hung up his coat. As he stared toward the kitchen, he could see the potatoes rapidly boiling and water spilling over the sides of the pan, and he found himself confused as to why I had left the supper unattended.

"Rachel! What are you doing?" David shouted from the bottom of the stairs.

"I'm in the bedroom, I'm just trying…" I had not even been able to finish explaining my predicament before the bedroom door swung open. Suddenly, David stood laughing at seeing my corset on backward, with my breasts barely able to remain inside the corset.

"I'm stuck, David! I can't move it round and I can't get it undone! It was supposed to be a surprise!"

As David stood in the doorway, he laughed so much that he could barely keep himself standing upright.

"It is a surprise all right!" David responded with a mocking tone. It had been such a long while since we had been able to laugh and feel free, especially about the issue of sex. We had never felt such contentment in the twelve years we had been married.

Trying for a Baby
People at work noticed that we looked happier, to such an extent that it almost became embarrassing, as neither of us would stop smiling. I was beginning to feel excited about the prospect of becoming pregnant, but at the same time I felt apprehensive about it. The emergency room where I was working had been busy one day, but I finally managed to sit down and take a bite of my lunch.

"That salad looks amazing, Rachel; did you make that?" Sarah, a heavily pregnant nurse, leaned over the table and studied my salad.

"Yes, David and I are on a healthy eating plan. So how are you doing anyway?"

"Great, only four more weeks to go and I will be meeting this little pumpkin," Sarah said while affectionately rubbing her enormous bump.

"Don't you feel scared, you know…of not having any control during the birth?" I asked, while crunching through a carrot.

"I think every woman feels a little apprehensive about the birthing experience, Rachel, but all I can think about is holding my beautiful child in my arms. Yes, I feel like I have no control over what my body is doing now, but even though I feel nauseated at times, full of gas and extremely constipated, I am full of happiness."

I knew that if I were to become pregnant, I would have little control over the experiences that pregnancy would bring with it. Deep beneath all my insecurities about being pregnant, I knew that I was more than ready to become a mom. Since I had overcome my vaginismus, the longing to have a baby had deeply intensified. For me, having a child was like adding the missing part of the jigsaw puzzle to a wonderful work of art. It was the greatest gift that any couple could be given, and I wanted David to experience that gift.

"So, are you guys planning on having a baby anytime soon then?" Sarah asked, while continuing to munch her sandwich. This question was the one question I had always dreaded being asked, but now I was happy and excited to answer that question.

"Yes, David and I have discussed having children a lot over the past couple of weeks and yes, we have made a commitment to each other to start trying for a baby."

"Oh, that's fantastic, Rachel! I am so excited for you guys! You and David will make great parents," Sarah said, smiling.

After returning home that evening, I kicked off my shoes and headed to the kitchen to make a drink. It had been a stressful and busy day in the emergency room and all I wanted was to sit in front of the TV with a nice glass of red wine. As I opened the pantry door, I suddenly remembered my promise to David to stop drinking alcohol.

"What I would give for a glass of red wine and some chocolate right now," I said as I plonked myself in front of the TV. David was already lying down watching TV and barely looked like he was awake.

"It will be worth it, Rachel, you'll see." I picked up the fertility book on the coffee table. This book had become my best friend, as I strictly followed its every command in the hope that I would increase my chance of becoming pregnant. Every day for three months I had strictly followed our baby-making schedule, and every month brought hope that this would be the month I would be pregnant. As I continued to read about the signs and symptoms of pregnancy and what we could do to enhance my chances, I had a sudden awareness that my breasts felt heavier and bigger than usual. I jumped up from the sofa and walked over to the bathroom mirror to further look for evidence that I might be pregnant.

"Hey, David, I think my nipples look darker than usual!" I studied myself in the bathroom mirror. As my eyes made their way down to my stomach, I was shocked to see it was bloated—proudly staring back at me from the bathroom mirror.

Am I finally pregnant? A wave of excitement rushed through my body.

The next morning, I made my way to the bathroom, more tired than usual and slightly nauseated. The time of the month that my period was to arrive was nearing and, as with every other previous month, I hoped that my period would not arrive. As I once again studied my body in the bathroom mirror, the waves of nausea intensified.

Surely, I am pregnant. My belly already looks as if I am carrying twins! As I made my way to work that morning, I continued to feel nauseated and different from how I had felt over the previous months. However, I felt happy and at peace about possibly being pregnant; it was a peace I had never before experienced.

After listening to the night nurse's report, Dr. Hadikie, a clean-shaven young surgeon, entered the staff room.

"Hello, ladies. Would one of you be free to chaperone a consult with me?"

"Sure, I'm free." I jumped up and followed the young doctor to his treatment room, where he carried out his consult with a plan to take this young lady to surgery. Her baby had spontaneously aborted itself that morning. As I stood in the treatment room, watching the young lady weep for the loss of her baby, I began to feel terrible. Here I was, possibly pregnant, standing at this lady's bedside during one of the darkest times of her life.

A few hours later, as I sat finishing up some charting, I suddenly began to feel period pains stronger than I had ever felt before. Waves of nausea swept over me as I quietly slipped off to the bathroom. *Am I going to be sick?*

Once in the stall, I saw it. My period. As I sat there on the hospital toilet, tears began to fill my eyes.

How could this be? I had been so sure that I was pregnant. How could I have experienced every possible symptom of pregnancy and not be pregnant?

I rushed home and cried with anger.

Why does my body have to play such sick jokes on me? Frustrated, I quickly reached for the bottle of red wine that was chilling in my fridge. After a few glasses of wine, its anesthetizing effects dulled my pain to a distant memory.

Month after month thereafter became a repeated experience of symptoms of pregnancy with failed pregnancy tests, and I began to feel my hopes of having a baby beginning to slip away.

I felt as though my disorder had already robbed years of my life. Never did I ever think that I would be middle-aged and childless. I found myself having a deep realization that time was running out on my biological clock. I could almost hear the ticking of the clock. I would be lying if I said that trying for a baby was not stressful for me. Although I had been cured of vaginismus, David and I were still finding sexual intercourse very mechanical and awkward from time to time, so we still often tended to avoid it. I had started to wonder if there was any way back for us—could we ever get over this?

We had lived together for so long as best friends, in a brother and sister relationship, and David often still found himself reverting to being my counselor. I know that David was having difficulty relaxing and relearning how to find sex enjoyable. And then, things slowly started to improve.

We started to make time for each other by taking time to go for a drink together or attending the cinema. We began to feel closer to each other. I started to really see how special David was, and how much I loved him. We spent time together on the weekends. We were having sex more often, and it grew more enjoyable. Now if we could just make a baby.

I stared intently at the fertility calendar displayed proudly on my kitchen wall. Another month had passed, and it had been three days since my period was supposed to arrive. However, this month I had felt unable to feel any sense of excitement at the thought that I might be pregnant. It was unusual for me to be late for my period, so I knew that the chance of my being pregnant was more of a possibility than previous months. I finally felt justified in peeing over a twenty-dollar piece of plastic. Those two minutes of waiting for the pregnancy test result were the longest two minutes I had ever passed. I glanced down at the results and stared in utter disbelief and shock at what I saw.

"Negative." Confused and overwhelmed with anger, I sat in the bathroom and cried. "Why? Have I not waited long enough?" I threw the negative pregnancy test into the waste bin. I stormed back into the kitchen, tears trickling down my face.

"Is it not enough that I have had to struggle for twelve years to overcome the effects of vaginismus? No! No, because now my body thinks that it is okay to play cruel tricks on me! How is this fair, David?"

"Negative again? You're right, Rachel, it's not fair. But life never is fair, is it?"

"I just don't understand, David. I thought after we had gotten over the vaginismus, everything would be okay. I never thought we would have issues with getting pregnant," I said.

David tried desperately to reassure me. "It's only been three months. We must keep trying. Some couples can take up to a year before they get pregnant; you know that."

Determined to find answers to why we were struggling to conceive, I grabbed the phone and dialed the medical center. I no longer felt worried about talking with health care professionals about my condition and I did not want to waste another minute.

"Hello, this is Rachel Louise. I really need to see a doctor as soon as possible." I could sense that the lady on the phone recognized my urgent need for help.

"What's the problem, Rachel?"

There was an awkward silence as I desperately tried to control my tears.

"I have been trying to get pregnant…and…something's not right. I have had so much happen over the years that is personal and has prevented me from being able to try for a baby—and well, I just don't think I can take any more of this pain. I really need to talk with a doctor." I was now in floods of tears.

After a few minutes of waiting for the medical receptionist to return to the phone, she replied, "Dear, could you be here by 2:30 p.m.? Your doctor has agreed to see you under the circumstances." The lady spoke with great empathy.

"Thank you. Thank you so much. Yes, I will be there," I said with relief as I hung up the phone.

That afternoon I walked into my doctor's office with red, puffy eyes and a trembling body.

Fertility Blues

"Hello, Rachel, what can I do for you today?" asked the friendly and polite doctor, who was also a colleague from the emergency department. He was an English doctor, and I had gotten to know him well over the years we had worked together. I didn't care about sharing my story anymore, as I no longer felt any shame from my disorder.

I began to share my story. "Well, David and I have been trying to get pregnant for quite a few months now and it seems that we are having problems. My periods are becoming more and more erratic and are now more often than not late, and I seem to be getting every symptom of pregnancy…I just don't understand why this is happening to me. I am doing everything the fertility books are telling me to do, and it's not working!"

Dr. Smith was fully aware of my long-standing history of vaginismus and Botox treatment.

"Rachel, you seem incredibly stressed, which is not going to help you conceive a baby. I do know how much you and David want this, but you have to find a way of managing the stress that you are experiencing around wanting a baby."

"But it's so frustrating, and I just feel so angry and so cheated. I cannot even look at a pregnant woman without feeling cheated anymore. I am just so tired of everything feeling like a constant battle—nothing can just be straightforward."

"Well, how about we do some blood tests and check that everything is okay, and I suggest you put those fertility books away and allow yourself some enjoyment with this process," Dr. Smith said while handing a lab form to me.

The doctor later informed me that my labs were clear and there were no abnormalities and absolutely no reason that I should not be able to get pregnant. I felt some relief but remained confused as to the reason it was taking so long.

As the months went by, I found I was becoming jealous of the women around me who were pregnant. As I entered the break room at work, I avoided talking about babies, which was difficult with everyone around me being pregnant. As I boiled the kettle to make some tea, I heard and watched the conversations and the laughter of the nurses.

"Do you have your nursery painted yet, Sally? I painted mine last week so now I just have to go and collect my baby crib from the store sometime next week," Sarah said to another pregnant nurse. It was a common sight to see two or three pregnant women with their feet up in the staff break room, and they all seemed to have developed a strong special bond.

"Hey, maybe I can come with you to pick up the crib and then we can go for lunch afterward." Sally continued to flip through a mother and baby catalog that was lying on the staff room table. As the kettle switched off, I made my tea and retreated to another part of the hospital. I had begun to do everything I could to avoid the break room. I did not want to listen to their happy stories of being pregnant and feel that I had to smile falsely to hide my true feelings. It began to feel like every other woman was becoming pregnant apart from me, and I was tired of the constant question, "Are you pregnant yet, Rachel?" I longed for the day that I could say yes to that question, but I was not sure that day would ever arrive.

During my breaks alone I would work on writing the words to the song that I'd started to write. I had sung since I was a young teenager, but I had never attempted to write a song. Part of me felt that I needed to find an outlet for the pain that I was unable to talk freely about. Music had always been a way for me to express such powerful emotions, and the songs were my way of expressing and removing the pain that I had felt. As I sat on my break writing the words to my song and humming the tune, I thought about how misunderstood I felt. People around me only saw quiet-natured Rachel, who never spoke openly about her sex life like others did or her desire to have children. I am sure many just thought I was strange or a snob.

David and I had been trying for a baby for a while now and still nothing. I had a strong feeling that something was very wrong. I knew that if I spoke up, people would say that I was overreacting--and much too soon. Deep down, I knew something just did not feel right.

Seed for Thought
"So do not fear, for I am with you; do not be dismayed, for I am your God" (Isaiah 41:10a).

CHAPTER TWELVE

A Big Sting in the Tail

"Marriage has no guarantees. If that's what you're looking for, go live with a car battery." —Erma Bombeck

"How's the song sounding, David?" I asked as I walked into the kitchen. David stood listening to music in his usual spot in the kitchen, while he prepared a ridiculously large meal that could have fed way more than two people.

"David, we are not going to eat ten potatoes, and why did you cook four chicken breasts?"

"Well, I'm hungry, and whatever we are unable to eat we can save and eat tomorrow," David said, smiling as if he had managed to outdo me in the argument. As I opened the fridge to get a drink, there was a big New York cheesecake staring back at me. As I turned and looked back at David, he began to smile and laugh, as he knew that I was thinking that he was a greedy pig. Our relationship was strong and playful.

"So, what do you think of my song?"

"It's coming along. You just need to keep practicing," David said.

"You think it's rubbish, don't you?"

"No! Not at all, Rachel! It just needs shaping a little more, that's all!"

I knew that my song was not to the standard I desired, so I continued to sing the words over and over, often with tears streaming down my face. Week after week I continued to work on my song.

Breaking My Silence
It had been around twelve months since I had overcome my vaginismus and I felt like I could conquer the world—like I had slayed a great dragon and overcome the major obstacles in my life. I was now at the point where I longed to find meaning for the suffering I had encountered. *What do I do with this suffering? It seems pointless to go through all this suffering if it has no purpose,* I thought.

    I began to think about ways I could help others who were suffering with vaginismus. I looked over the song I had worked on in the basement at my old house while living in a small, isolated town in British Columbia. I had written this song during some of the darkest days of my life. Around twelve months after being cured, David and I moved to a larger Canadian city which was about a nine-hour drive southeast from where we were living. We had lived in the small oil and gas town for a around three years and we needed to get away from the small town for a while. The small-town living had given us time out of the rat race to focus on curing my condition, but now we felt claustrophobic and hemmed in. Everywhere we looked it seemed like everyone was pregnant or trying for a baby and the pressure to get pregnant just became far too intense. David and I both got full-time jobs at the hospital and a cute two-bedroom house in an affluent part of the downtown core of the city. It felt good to start afresh and recreate our lives once again and leave behind the pain of vaginismus.

    As I stared down at my song, I smiled to myself as I thought back to one of those days that I had been working on it. Finally, my song was finished. I could not do anything else with it, and I was not sure what I was to do with it.

    As I glanced over at my piano, a crazy idea entered my mind of using the song I had written over a year ago about my experience with vaginismus. The thought of using my very own song about my personal experiences encouraged me. Writing a song and sharing my story felt like a way that I could reclaim my victory and at the same time would comfort others who were still battling vaginismus. The next thing I knew, David and I sat outside a recording studio with my song in my hand, waiting to meet a music producer who had agreed to listen to my song.

"David, what if he laughs at my song? What if he thinks it's rubbish?" I asked. The palms of my hands were sweaty. My heart raced with nervous anticipation, and I suddenly felt sick with panic.

"You're here now, Rachel! You have wanted to do this for months! You wrote that song for a reason, so why not just see what happens?" David replied, as he got out of the truck and rang the studio doorbell.

As the door opened, I was greeted by a trendy and good-looking young man who welcomed us into his studio. At this point, I began to have a dialogue in my head once again and thought, *Fantastic, now I have to sit and share my personal song with a young man who is probably going to think it is weird and will surely think that I am a freak!*

However, the producer simply said, "Well, show me what you've got then!" as he pointed to the piano in the studio. As I sat down, he pulled his stool up beside me and grabbed his guitar, a pencil and some paper.

In my insecurity, I blurted, "I am not good at playing the piano, you know, and this is my first ever song that I have written. I just want you to know that it might not be good!" The producer calmly reassured me that it could not be any worse than some of the crazy stuff that he had heard in his studio.

"Okay, then! Here it is!" I said nervously and sang the song while he played the music on his expensive guitar.

> When you look at me,
> what do you see?
> Do you see somebody happy?
> Or do you see somebody sweet?
>
> Am I someone you can laugh at?
> Or am I someone you don't see?
> Or are there innocent scars,
> all over me?
>
> You don't have to be afraid anymore!
> You don't have to hide away in this fortress.
> You're not alone anymore,

so dry your eyes and break those ties.
You don't have to be alone anymore.
You don't have to be alone anymore.

You say I'm too quiet,
too serious for you,
should stand up for myself
and open up my world to you.

Every day I am in conflict
with the reason for my existence,
so forgive me
for creating an illusion of me.

You don't have to be alone anymore!
You don't have to be alone anymore.

You don't have to hide away in this fortress.
You're not alone anymore,
so dry your eyes and break those ties.
You don't have to be alone anymore.

I grieved in silence,
with a smile on my face.
Hoping no one discovered,
this fake portrait I had made.
Oh, alcohol seems to be my only escape.
From the honeymoon memories
that still run right through my veins.

You don't have to be afraid anymore!
You don't have to hide away in this fortress.
You're not alone anymore,
so dry your eyes and break those ties.
You don't have to be alone anymore.
You don't have to be alone anymore.

As I finished my song, I felt exposed—like I had finally told someone my personal story of suffering with vaginismus. I waited for the producer to ask what my song was about or to look awkwardly embarrassed. Instead, he began to sing my song back to me while he strummed his guitar, and it was at that point I realized that he was taking my song seriously. I realized that I had actually written a song that I could record. He continued to sing my song, and we sat for a few hours rearranging it and singing it over and over until it was ready.

"Right! My afternoon is free! So how about we record a sketch of the song?" he asked, as he began to set up the microphones. Once everything was set up and I was singing in front of the producer, it was as if everything finally made sense.

The next few weeks were amazing. I hummed my song at work, and I sang it over and over at home until the recording was finally completed at the studio. The producer handed me the headphones and I listened to my song in its completed form for the first time. I was amazed at the outcome of my first-ever song. I felt so elated at that point, that I finally felt strong, like I had survived my storm and my life had finally turned around for the better.

I no longer felt the loneliness, isolation or despair I had felt over the previous months. I felt that I had finally gotten my joy back. It was a good thing, because I would need that joy to carry me through the next step in our journey toward a family.

A Big Sting

After finishing a long day at work a few days later, I jumped into the truck and David informed me that my gynecologist had left a message to contact her at her office. I knew very well that gynecologists did not phone you at home without reason. After numerous attempts to follow up the phone call with my gynecologist, I finally gave up, and then one afternoon she phoned me at work.

"Phone call for Rachel on extension 1239."

As I picked up the phone, I heard the voice of my gynecologist on the line. "Oh, hello, Rachel! I am so sorry that it has taken so long for us to reconnect. I have had a lot of trouble getting through to you for some reason. Anyway, do you have a few moments to talk?"

I looked around at the busy staff room, which was full of nurses munching their supper while the TV commercials blared out.

"Yes, of course," I said, knowing that I wouldn't get another chance to talk with her for a while if I declined the opportunity.

"Well, the good news, Rachel, is that your ultrasound shows that you have young and healthy ovaries and your lab work looks normal. However, there seems to be a problem with David." She paused for a few seconds. "Our tests show that he is not producing any sperm at all."

As soon as she said this, I could feel my stomach churning and my heart begin to race. As I sat in the crowded staff room, I felt as though someone had just punched me in the stomach. I did not expect David to have any problems. The thought had never crossed my mind. I jumped up from my seat and ran into the hospital corridor so that I could speak openly. "Does that mean he is infertile?" I quietly inquired, already knowing the answer.

"Yes, I am afraid so, Rachel. David cannot have children. I am so sorry to have to tell you this."

After discussing appointments and fertility clinic referrals, I put the phone down in shock. Suddenly, I felt numb and everything in me just wanted to have a meltdown and cry. As I stood in the hospital corridor, I dialed my home number, and David quickly answered. I knew that he would pick up the phone quickly, as he is used to me calling him on my breaks for a quick chat.

"Hello," he said, with Jasper the cat whining in the background. Everything in me wanted to reject sharing this devastating news with David over the phone. However, I was so upset, and I knew that I needed to speak to someone.

"Hey, how's it going?" I asked, as I tried to sensitively tell my husband after all his years of loyalty to me, that he was infertile.

"The gynecologist phoned for you, Rachel. Did she manage to contact you at work?" David asked, eagerly wanting to know what was going on. Both of us believed that if anything were going to go wrong with anyone, it would have gone wrong for me. It had never entered our minds that it would be David who had an issue.

"Yeah, I just got off the phone with her! I am afraid I have some really bad news, David!" I paused and David was silent as he waited for me to continue. I heard David sigh, and I could sense his dread as to what I was going to share. "She said that you have no sperm at all, which sadly means that you are infertile!"

As I explained to David what the gynecologist had said, I felt like my heart was being ripped out of my chest. I felt so upset that during all those years of struggling with vaginismus, David had faithfully done the right thing and remained by my side. This was how he was repaid by God for his loyalty?

"I have no sperm? Why? That cannot be right! She said that I had no sperm at all?" The sound of David's voice jolted me back from my thoughts, as I heard the shock and disbelief in his voice.

"She has referred us to speak with a consultant at the IVF (in vitro fertilization) clinic so we can find out what our options are. I guess they will do more tests to see if they can find out what the issue is."

"I don't understand. I just can't believe this, Rachel." David sounded annoyed and frustrated with the news. I could hear the sadness in his voice.

"I am so sorry to tell you this news, David. The gynecologist felt that the news would be better coming from me. I know how much you want kids, David. I don't understand this either, but we will get through this."

"I know, Rachel, but it's just another thing to contend with when I thought everything was finally fixed."

"I know. We can get a second opinion, though. Maybe she has got it wrong. Maybe its fixable." I quickly looked at my watch and realized my break had been long over.

"I should get back to work before they send a search party! I will talk with you when I get home."

I knew that it was not the best time to talk with David about infertility during a telephone call. But at the same time, I wanted him to have some time to let this news sink in before we met up. I knew that he would be picking me up from work in one hour and that he would be over the initial shock by that time. I knew that when he arrived, we would again be able to talk about our future. I returned to work with my heart breaking for David. I knew now that it was my time to be strong. David had been so strong during my difficulties, and now it was time for me to support him.

UNBROKEN LOVE

As I walked back into the unit and the busyness of the emergency department, I knew that I had to leave my personal issues at the door. There was no room for crying or having a meltdown right now. I had sick patients who needed my undivided attention. I guess this would be my life from now on anyway, living to show up to work every day. I officially could not have a child with David that we could call our own.

Two Peas in a Pod
Not long thereafter, we visited the infertility clinic. As I walked into the clinic, I saw white coats everywhere. I looked around the waiting room and all I saw was pictures of babies on the wall.

"How insensitive is that?" David blurted in his usual blunt way. "This is a fertility clinic where people are trying to get pregnant, and they put babies on the wall—how insensitive are these people?" He continued to mutter under his breath.

"Rachel and David!" the nurse shouted and pointed for us to follow her into a room to wait for the doctor. As she closed the door behind her, I looked around at the cold clinical room and I again started to feel an overwhelming sense of isolation, emptiness and hopelessness. I had thought that I had seen my last doctor's office after I had received the Botox treatment in Manchester, New Hampshire. I really did not expect to be sitting waiting to see another specialist two years down the line.

I felt so confused and again that question kept circling my head, *Why? Why...why?* If I could only find the answer to my question—why? I think both David and I would have been able to accept that we were going to live a childless life if we just knew the reasons why.

Did God think we would make terrible parents? Was I going to die early in life? Was our child going to turn out a psychopath? Not knowing the reasons left me in a constant state of confusion. I felt disillusioned with my life and once again I began to be reminded of the familiar feeling of a loss of identity in the world. Where did I fit now, and what was my purpose for being on this earth?

In a twisted sort of way, I started to laugh at the fact that David and I had sought each other out from among the billions of people on this earth. I mean, what are the odds of a woman with vaginismus finding a man who is infertile? That was a miracle. Sadly, the miracle that we so desperately prayed for never seemed to happen. But God gave us each other for a reason. After the specialist examined David and explained our options, he gave us a stack of lab requisitions for ultrasounds, blood work and X-rays.

"David, after examining you, I think you may have a blockage. That is what I am currently leaning toward now, but the lab work and ultrasound will confirm this."

The doctor moved his eyes from David toward me and continued. "I am afraid that even if David does have a blockage, your only option would be IVF or sperm donation. I am so deeply sorry, but please know that we will do everything we can to help you guys have a baby."

I sat listening with a sense of hope but also a sense of despair. I really detested the idea of having to go on yet another long roller-coaster journey of fighting against the odds only to once again find that we are checkmated in the game of life.

Part of me thought it would just be easier to close the door and move on with our lives. I looked at the doctor, who was busy filling out mountains of forms on our behalf. His gleaming white lab coat in the cold, empty clinical room made me wonder even further why I was asking my next question.

"How much does IVF cost?" I asked, knowing that we could not afford the money anyway.

"Fifteen thousand dollars is the initial cost of IVF. Then for every other embryo we defrost, it will be around two thousand dollars for each subsequent round." I smiled at the doctor and thanked him for his time.

Deep down I was already feeling that IVF was a closed door for us. We were still trying to climb out of the debt we had for the Botox treatment two years earlier. I was also aware that we needed to save a deposit for our own house. How could we justify spending another eleven to fifteen thousand dollars on treatment that might not even be successful when we did not even have the money to pay for a simple, much-deserved vacation? It had been a long journey trying to climb out of our debt, and we were still working hard to pay it off now.

Tough Decisions

David and I had not felt like we had experienced a vacation since we got married. We had visited Canada on a few occasions, but we spent our time either completing missions work or finding out about prospective nursing jobs. Even if we had booked a beach vacation, it would never have felt like a break, as everywhere we went, we took our issue with us. Now that we were just feeling like we were getting on top again, we found that we might have to go back into debt if we wanted to take one last risk to try to open a door that seemed to be so very tightly closed. David and I had a lot of tough decisions to make, and we both knew that this would not be an easy one.

A few weeks later, David and I found ourselves sitting once again in the cold clinical doctor's office waiting to find out the results of our tests for IVF treatment. The room always seemed so quiet and peaceful but at the same time lonely. The wait for the doctor to arrive with the results of our tests seemed to be endless.

"I am going to have to go and put more money in the meter if they don't hurry up," David said, showing his annoyance at having to wait such a long time for the doctor.

Suddenly there was a faint knock at the door and the doctor with the gleaming white coat and perfect set of white teeth entered the room.

"Hello again, guys," the doctor said while shaking our hands. He immediately opened his laptop and started to share our results. After a long explanation of technical terms he was using about David being blocked and there possibly being a production problem, he stopped and said, "In a nutshell, you guys are about as complicated as it gets. You are the complicated case study that every doctor dreads having to answer on their exam sheet."

I do not believe for a second that his intention was to be cruel; his face appeared to be genuine and concerned. He was being truly honest, and he was clearly telling us that if we chose the IVF treatment, there was only a very slim chance that I would get pregnant from David. That is, if IVF was even an option for us and this still had to be determined through more tests.

There would still be numerous tests and examinations that David would need to undergo before we could even know if IVF was possible for us. If David had no sperm hiding in his testicles, then again it would be game over. Thirteen years ago, I would never have dreamed that I would be sitting in front of an IVF specialist. After finally overcoming a long and painful journey with vaginismus, it never crossed my mind for a second that David would be infertile. I never saw myself as childless either. I hated what I knew I had to say to David, but I knew deep in my heart that it was the right decision. Nobody ever said that making the right decision would never be painful.

"David, I have been thinking and I really don't think it's the best decision for us to go down the IVF route. What do you think?" I said hesitantly as we drove home in our truck.

"As much as I hate to admit it, Rachel, I think I agree. I really would love children of my own, but I am starting to believe that it's just not meant to be."

As we drove back to our house, we sat quietly, almost in a state of realization that our journey of trying for our own children had finally come to an end. After discussing all of the positives and negatives for IVF, the writing seemed to be on the wall. We were never going to have children of our own.

Once home, I sat alone on the side of the bathtub with the door closed. Tears streamed down my face. Although I felt at peace with our decision not to proceed with having biological children, it did not stop me from feeling the deep sense of loss and grief that I would never experience what it felt like to be pregnant or have a child that was created by David and me. Reality had suddenly hit me—I was thirty-five years old and at the end of time on my biological clock with no children, and my family and friends were all overseas. I looked in the mirror and I no longer saw a fresh-looking twenty-year-old full of life. Instead, I saw a middle-aged woman with wrinkles around her eyes. David had always longed to be a father and again it was something else that God seemed to have closed the door on. Even though I knew we were making the right decision, it didn't stop me from crying out to Him and asking Him why.

"Why, God…why?" I cried. I just could not understand the point of this pain.

As the reality of what my future was going to hold hit me, I slid to the floor as if all the energy in my body had just been sucked right out of me. At that point, enough was truly enough. How could I continue to believe in a God who would allow me to experience this much pain and suffering? In a very impolite manner, I told the God who had been a significant part of my life from the age of four years old to leave me.

I was so angry that my relationship with Him had been left in tatters. I had been robbed of having children. I felt almost a relief for ridding myself of the religion that had controlled my life. I knew it was time that God showed me He was real and that He cared about me.

As I calmed down from my outburst, I felt a pang of guilt that I was complaining about my life when I knew there were others far worse off than me. I still had my physical health, full-time employment and a husband who loved me and was devoted to me. I had a lot to be thankful for. As I sat alone in the early hours of the morning, I told God I was sorry, but I asked that He allow me time to rediscover my faith in Him for myself.

I no longer wanted to just believe in God because that was what I had been taught to believe all my life. I had to know if God was real for myself. Part of me wondered if I would still find out that God was real, or if I would discover that God was just a mere fantasy or myth that I had been taught to believe was true from the time I was a child.

Surprise Infertility *(David's Perspective)*
I remember wondering why Rachel had not conceived yet. We had been trying for a child of our own for some time, but nothing seemed to be happening. So, we went to see our family physician and ended up being referred to a fertility clinic. After having undergone a series of tests, a few weeks later I learned that I was infertile. I was quite stunned at that point.

We had been through so much together already and had managed to get a breakthrough with the sexual disorder side of things, and now it felt like some kind of sick joke. For years, I had avoided the discussions about adoption with Rachel and stated, "I want to have our own children!" Isn't it amazing how things work out in life? We can presume to do this, that or the next thing. We attempt to plan our lives out with what we want and what we don't want. Yet, sometimes, our master plans are interrupted and grind to a halt.

After the initial disappointment, I approached our infertility matter with a very simple outlook and radically accepted the hand of cards I had been dealt. In a way, it was a relief to just accept it, because I knew that it would be futile to lock horns with the universe! It must have taken me less than twenty-four hours to heartily accept our predicament with respect to having our own children. At that point, I became genuinely open to the prospect of adopting children.

Seed for Thought
"There is a time for everything, and a season for every activity under heaven: a time to be born and a time to die, a time to plant and a time to uproot, a time to kill and a time to heal, a time to tear down and a time to build, a time to weep and a time to laugh, a time to mourn and a time to dance, a time to scatter stones and a time to gather them, a time to embrace and a time to refrain, a time to search and a time to give up, a time to keep and a time to throw away, a time to tear and a time to mend, a time to be silent and a time to speak, a time to love and a time to hate, a time for war and a time for peace" (Ecclesiastes 3:1–8).

SECTION THREE

Flowers

CHAPTER THIRTEEN

A New Journey
With David's Perspective

"When you understand that life is a test, you realize that nothing is insignificant in your life." —Rick Warren

It was not long before David and I were attending a preadoption meeting in the northeast side of the city where we lived in Canada. It was around six months after contemplating IVF treatment, and we had both decided that adoption seemed to be the way forward.

"David, you have gone the wrong way," I moaned as David chose to ignore the GPS loudly communicating to us to go left.

"She's wrong, Rachel. I am sure that the office is down this street," David said insistently.

"You're saying that the GPS has got it wrong," I said sarcastically. As we drove in the opposite direction from what the GPS was instructing us to do, we soon realized that we were heading in the wrong direction.

"See, I told you, David, we are meant to be over there." I pointed over to an array of shops that the GPS was directing us toward.

"Rachel, how can a social service agency be among an array of shops like Canadian Tire and Wal-Mart? It seems illogical that a social service office would be placed there." David continued to argue his point that the GPS instructions were wrong. As we pulled into the parking lot outside Canadian Tire, sure enough, we saw the social service agency right in front of us.

"See, if you had just trusted the GPS, we would have gotten here ages ago," I said, smiling that I had won the argument. It had been three years since I had received my Botox treatment and six months since I had attended the IVF clinic. We found ourselves on quite a different venture from what we had imagined fourteen years ago.

As we stepped out of our truck and walked toward the social service office, I started to feel a little nervous. David and I had decided to attend an adoption introduction evening to inquire more about how we could adopt a waiting child from the system.

Accepting Our Situation

It was not an easy decision for us to make, as we had both expected that we would eventually have children of our own one day. Closing the door on the slim possibility of IVF treatment being successful was one of the most difficult decisions we have ever had to make. However, sometimes the paths that we find ourselves on in life do not always seem to make perfect sense—like the social service agency being located among the shops seemed illogical. It made no sense to us but that is where the building was located, and we did not have the power to change that. We had to learn to accept our situation and keep moving forward.

"Hello, we are here for the adoption introduction," I said nervously. A slim, pretty brunette lady directed us to the room where the talk was taking place. As we entered the room, we were amazed that it was full of couples like us who were interested in adopting a child. It was reassuring to see so many couples from all different walks of life following the alternative route of creating a family.

We met so many wonderful couples through our adoption meetings, some of whom have become lifelong friends. As David and I listened to the social workers talk about some of the children they had in their care and what it takes to adopt, I realized that we were being geared up for a whole new journey. From applying for a child to finally adopting a child could take at least two to three years.

"We are going to be so old, David, when we finally get a child," I whispered.

I knew that adoption was a tough and lengthy process, but I was unaware of how long the process could take. However, it did not dissuade us from our decision to proceed with adopting. As I continued to listen to the social workers, I was reminded of my own childhood and how my parents fostered children throughout most of my childhood years.

As I thought back to the days I lived at the children's home and school, I was reminded of all the children who went through our care. They were some of the happiest times in my life, living in that children's home. It was only after the home closed and my family had to move to subsidized housing that life started to become unhappy for us. Thinking back to all that God had taken David and me through, I felt that God had been preparing, equipping and setting us aside for an extremely important role.

If David had remained in ministry, he would never have trained as a mental health nurse. If we had not immigrated to Canada, we would not be sitting in the meeting that day. If I had not gone through the pain of vaginismus and David's infertility, we likely would not be considering adoption as an option.

Even back in my childhood, God had already started preparing and equipping me to become a mother to children who had experienced loss and grief themselves—the loss of their family, their identity and personhood and certainly a big loss of control and security. David had developed so many skills in caring for children with mental health needs and had also experienced a lot of trauma and abuse himself, so he was no stranger to facing challenges and pain.

I thought back to how the children would initially hide or behave badly toward us. I remembered one young boy taking a dislike to me as soon as he set foot in our home. He would shout at me to leave him alone, and I remembered being confused as to why he was being so nasty, when all I was trying to do was be nice.

Having a Voice *(David's Perspective)*

As we listened to the social worker deliver her speech, she finally invited all those attending to ask any questions and make any comments.

Seizing the opportunity, I immediately stated, "You guys are going to take one look at my resume, and your eyes are going to light up when you see my employment history! But please don't assume that because I work with severely challenging behavior, I would want to come home to the same thing every day!"

The silence was deafening, and then some people started to laugh when I unpacked my statement even further. In essence, my experience with addictions, forensic mental health and acute mental health was not going to be a license for social services to work their magic and leave Rachel and me with a kid like Michael Myers from the movie *Halloween*!

After I had made my point, the social worker validated my concerns and further reassured me that Rachel and I would not be approached with any particular children on the mere basis of our employment experience.

I felt frustrated as I sat there, as I was thinking about my own former lifestyle with drug abuse, criminal behavior and homelessness. It was not the fault of the other people who were attending this meeting, but I really wasn't trying to be funny. I was serious because I knew the lifestyle that I came out of. I knew the lifestyle of those clients with whom I worked daily. I knew the lifestyle of the parents, who were at the end of their rope. So, although my comments may have been funny on a superficial level, I really wasn't laughing at all. I was scared, and I did not fully accept or trust the validation and reassurance that came from the speaker that evening.

Introductory Meetings

A few weeks after our introductory meeting with the social workers, I was sitting in my lounge looking at comments on Facebook. I had just completed my music video and I was looking at the photos of the filming and the comments people had placed. As I continued to flick through the photos, the phone rang. *Probably David phoning me from work as he usually does.*

"Hello?"

"Hello, is this Rachel?" the lady asked.

"Yes, this is Rachel."

"Rachel, this is the social worker regarding your application to adopt. When can I come and see you?"

The social workers had earlier informed us at the introductory meeting that it would take at least four weeks until they would contact us. It had been barely a week when she contacted us, so I was caught a little by surprise. As we set up our meeting for the following week, I realized that proceeding with adoption had now become our new and exciting journey.

As I hung up the phone, I started to wonder what our children would be like. It was strange to think that our children were living their life somewhere and that we were yet to meet. David and I had decided to set a few boundaries on age and had decided to look at taking on a sibling group. We could potentially be asked to adopt a child from the age of newborn to twelve years of age.

(David's Perspective)
Approximately one week later, Rachel received a telephone call from social services that resulted in the arranging of a psychologist to come and assess us over a two-day period. The psychologist was approved by social services and served the purpose of undertaking preadoption assessments in order to establish an appropriate match between ourselves and potential adoptees. I think it was about two or three months later when we had the psychologist in our home. She appeared to be very straitlaced and wanted to get right down to business. Her formal and seemingly cold approach made me think, *Great! Wait until she digs into my past life of serious drug abuse!*

To my surprise, during this grueling assessment of my former drug-abusing lifestyle, the psychologist did not convey any judgment or discrimination in her facial expressions, tone of voice or body language. I was very calm in my approach as I responded to her many questions, but I was also watching her every move. She won my approval as I studied her calm rate, tone and pitch of speech. She won my approval as I quickly examined her authentic facial expressions and body language responses. And she won my approval when she conveyed a sense of humanity that far surpassed the initial straitlaced and formal "get down to business" appearance.

After all was said and done, we politely shook hands, and that was that. However, it was not long before we were assigned a social worker, who would work with Rachel and me on an ongoing basis about our adoption pursuits. Charlotte was a young and pretty midtwenties social worker. Although I liked her, I was also wary about her youthfulness and the fact that she was not a parent to any children.

Without any disrespect toward Charlotte, I wrongly began to think, *How can she advise someone like me, with my crazy background, about adopting kids into our home?* However, I quickly realized that I was being defensive because of my own fears and insecurities. Charlotte was a wise young woman for whom I have utmost respect. She visited Rachel and me on a regular basis and won our confidence.

A New Dream
I sat and thought about how our children were possibly living their lives somewhere else while we carried on our lives until we were matched. I started to take notice of the children around me, and I began to analyze my reactions to children of different ages.

It no longer seemed to bother me like it used to when I looked at a pregnant woman or saw a baby. I had realized and come to terms with the reality that I was not going to be carrying a child of my own, not in my womb, anyway. But I would have arms to carry children and to provide plenty of hugs. Instead, I was going to become a mom to some children who so very much needed a mom.

As I sat and thought about our new beginning, I knew that the path we were choosing was the right path. Our path and our thoughts are not always God's thoughts. It is difficult to see where God is going sometimes, as it often does not seem to make much sense. I remember when I was in the midst of all the pain and feeling I had lost all hope and was ready to end my life. I was convinced that God had forgotten us, and I could see no purpose for my life.

But as I sat listening to the social workers chat about the different children and the needs they had, I felt like I had come home. I knew that we had been set apart for this task. This was our purpose. God does not always choose to do miracles in the way that we expect them. He sometimes chooses to give us miracles that we could never have imagined possible.

David and I had time to spend with each other while we waited for our children. We had faced many tornados in life and each one left its path of destruction. However, each time we have been faced with a tornado, we have refused to give in, and we have continued to move forward. Each time we have worked our way through the destruction, and our marriage has become stronger.

While we undertook the journey of adoption, we also concentrated on having some fun. We were taking a journey back to New York and Boston the coming fall, as we now saw this as the place where our marriage was given a chance to blossom. New York had been the place where my vaginismus ended and my new journey with David started. No longer were we plagued by vaginismus, which was holding our relationship back. New York had become our second honeymoon destination where there are no bad memories. Our first honeymoon in Spain was a place that held nothing but bad memories, as we had been unable to move past the vaginismus.

When David and I spent time with each other, there were no longer any pressures in the bedroom. We were not having sex to solve a problem or to make a baby, but because we loved each other. Sex was no longer about pain but about having fun and showing each other true love.

Wheels in Motion *(David's Perspective)*
One day, Charlotte visited us and told us "We have a match for you guys!" This freaked me out! Here we were, a couple who had been married for fourteen years, a couple who had experienced major psychosexual problems and had no clue about being parents, and here we were on the brink of having children! Charlotte said, "You've been matched to a sibling group, a little five-year-old boy and his six-year-old sister."

It felt very surreal. All of a sudden we were going to potentially become the parents of two children, who already had a biological mom and dad. A ready-made family was in the cards now. I had already faced the infertility cards a few months earlier. Now I was facing the cards of being a father to two kids who had a lot of history.

Charlotte explained that our psychological assessment had been formulated into a report, which was sent to the main adoption headquarters. Our profile had been matched to Jake and Jessica, who were both born and initially raised in Canada.

Within weeks, Rachel and I attended an information-sharing meeting, where the foster parents of Jake and Jessica also attended and answered any questions that Rachel and I had. We wrote down lots of notes, and it was only a matter of two or three weeks before we met the kids at their different foster homes. Although Jake and Jessica were biological siblings, they had been raised in separate foster homes about twenty-four miles apart. Rachel and I were introduced to Jake and Jessica at their foster homes, and we met them on different occasions over the next few weeks. We could not have imagined what our journey would entail when we set out on it, but looking back, we saw that we were perfectly made for one another, and our trials made us stronger. Rachel even came to realize that she was created to be the mom of just the right children…who were soon to arrive.

Seed for Thought
"'For my thoughts are not your thoughts, neither are your ways my ways,' declares the Lord" (Isaiah 55:8).

CHAPTER FOURTEEN

Growing a Family
With David's Perspective

"Every flower must grow through dirt." —Laurie Sennott

"I'm nervous, David; I feel like my stomach is doing somersaults." It was nearing 2:00 p.m. and David had just pulled up outside the house where we would meet our son for the second time, only this time we were taking him and his sister out for a few hours.

"Shall we go knock on the door then?" David said, as he impatiently jumped out of his truck. As I sat nervously in the truck, I looked at the booster seats in the back seat of the truck. *This really is happening*, I thought.

"Rachel! We are going to be late! Come on!"

David opened the passenger door. As I jumped out of the truck, I reminisced about the first time we had met our son and daughter. We had to meet them separately. The children had been fostered separately for four years and only saw each other monthly.

As we walked toward the front door, I smiled. I remembered my daughter standing with a piece of paper in her hands, dressed in bib overalls, standing close to her social worker. She nervously looked around the room. Her hair was curly, long and neatly tied up in a ponytail, and she had recently turned six.

Jessica lit up the room with her radiant smile, and her mischievous personality could be seen by the way that she peered over the glasses that kept slipping down her face or becoming lopsided.

David turned to me and smiled. "She's so cute, Rachel!"

After sitting down on the sofa, Jessica stood and read the questions from her crumpled piece of paper.

"Do you like rice?" she asked nervously. David and I looked at each other and smiled.

"We love rice, don't we, David! We eat rice all the time!"

Her face lit up as she turned to her foster mom and smiled. "Did you hear that! They like rice, Mom!" Jessica had lived with her foster mom since she was two years old and had learned to call her Mom. I worried that she would find the transition of calling me Mom difficult.

After spending a few hours with Jessica, David and I had to travel forty minutes outside of the city to meet our son, Jake. As I walked up the front path to my son's foster care house, the door quickly swung open and there, sitting on the floor, was Jake. His foster mom was standing over him and trying to remove a bag from him. His cheeks were bright red, and overgrown strawberry-blond curls fell over his face. Jake sat at the front door with a suitcase by his side.

"Are we going now? I have my suitcase ready." He grabbed his suitcase and started to stand up.

When we had first visited Jake, he started to pack his suitcase with clothes and toys.

"I don't live here anymore; I am moving to a new house. I am coming to live at your house," he said while pulling all of his clothes from closets and drawers. There were so many teddy bears that it seemed that it would be impossible for them to fit into such a small case. He told me only one teddy was special to him and he could never leave that one behind. That was the teddy his birth mom had given him. It was the first time that we had met Jake and it seemed so strange to watch a child so young process his adoption by packing his bag on the first day we had met him.

His foster mom was trying to explain for a second time that he was only going out for a few hours and then returning back to his foster home.

"But I am moving to a new house! This isn't my house now." Jake seemed anxious and confused.

"That's right, Jake, but today we are taking you out somewhere special and then…" Jake suddenly bolted from the front door and back to his room. "I need my dinosaur! Where's my dinosaur?" he said, as he ran back to his bedroom.

David and I knew that parenting two children who had not had the best start in life would be a steep learning curve. Both children had learned that people they love leave them. Nothing in life had been constant for them, and they both had to learn to trust again.

Although we were both a little scared, at the same time we were extremely excited about becoming parents to two incredibly special little beings. We had decorated their rooms and purchased beds, new clothes and toys. Everything was ready for them to move to our house in ten days' time. The transition was quick, and we had to gain their trust in a very short time.

***

Today is going to be a great day, I thought. We had arranged to take our new son and daughter to a place known as Chuck E. Cheese. It seemed to be every young child's dream in Canada: endless junk food, candy and games where they won toys. Children loved visiting Chuck E. Cheese, so we were looking forward to taking our new son and daughter somewhere special.

After securing our son in his booster seat, we were on the road heading to collect Jessica. The journey took around forty minutes from the city where we were living in Canada. As we drove along the road to collect our daughter, I took a quick peek at my son through my visor mirror. *This is actually happening; I am finally going to be a mom!* I thought. As I sat staring into dreamland, I was suddenly jolted back to reality by a booming loud voice from the back seat.

"Rachel! Rachel!"

Jake sat bolt upright in his booster seat, and his eyes were fixated on me as he began to fire questions at me. His speech was difficult to understand when we first met, and he struggled to pronounce a lot of words. For the whole forty-minute journey, Jake spoke and asked questions until we reached Jessica's house. If I turned and attempted to talk with David, Jake would start calling my name and demand my attention.

"Are we getting Jessica now? Is Jessica going to be living with me? What about Lynne? Will I see her again?"

Lynne had fostered Jake for about two years and doted on him. She was in her sixties and alone, so she was unable to adopt him. I watched her tear up when she spoke at the meeting we had before we had met Jake and Jessica.

"Whatever you do, don't watch him eat! He gets food everywhere, all up his arms and all over his face. If you look at him when he eats, he will cover himself even more." She had managed a lot of Jake's challenging behaviors alone and knew that as he grew older, she would not be able to manage him by herself. Jake had learned a variety of swear words by the time he was two years old.

As we turned onto the street to collect Jessica, my stomach did another somersault. I constantly worried about Jessica not liking me. *What if I am not good enough to be her mom?* She seemed so perfect and loved dressing up as an angel and pretending to make tea and cakes.

I felt so honored to be Jake and Jessica's mom, but I knew they both needed so much more than average parenting—they needed unconditional love, a love unbreakable. David and I knew we had the ability to fight a challenge, and although we knew we were blessed to have two wonderful children, we also knew there would be many challenges along the way.

As the truck pulled up at Jessica's house, she was already waiting at the front door. She quickly ran to the truck, got herself into her booster seat, and secured her seat belt. She turned to her brother and smiled. "Hi, Jake!"

It was not until a few years later that Jessica confided that she had not known that Jake was her brother until the adoption process started. She only got to visit him once a month and she just thought she was supposed to be friends with him.

"Chuck E. Cheese! Chuck E. Cheese! Chuck E. Cheese! Eeeeek!" Jessica and Jake screamed as we pulled up outside. David and I had no idea what Chuck E. Cheese was, and it certainly ended up testing our parenting skills.

The children ran from game to game and filled themselves up with pop and junk food. As the afternoon went on, it seemed that Jake became redder and hotter. When we said it was time to leave Chuck E. Cheese, he looked like a sweaty little tomato.

"Okay, kids, it's time to go," David shouted as he looked toward the top of the slide where the kids were both sitting. Jessica and Jake stared back from the enclosed bubble above the slide and mischievously giggled and continued to play with the other children. Every few minutes they would shout our names from the enclosed bubble and wave to us. David and I knew we were now being held hostage by a five-year-old and a six-year-old. They knew that they were unreachable, enclosed in the plastic bubble.

"Okay…now what, David? What do we do when they ignore us?"

"Let's just give them a few minutes, Rachel. They have got to come down sooner or later."

It was our first outing as a family, and we were trying to avoid power struggles. Minutes later, Jessica suddenly flew out of the slide. Feeling a sense of hope, I stood up and walked over to the slide. Seeing me heading toward her, she quickly ran back toward the stairs in an attempt to climb back into the bubble. Jake was still standing in the bubble, frantically banging on the plastic to get our attention. Before she could climb the stairs, I quickly grabbed her by the straps of her bib overalls.

"Not so fast, Jessica, we have to go now. We have to get you home, or people will be worried about you." She turned and looked at me. Her face was also looking hot and red.

"But me and Jake are having so much fun, we don't want to go yet. Can we stay? Please…please, can we stay a little longer? Please!" she pleaded.

"Jessica, we can come again, I promise. Now can you please go tell your brother that he needs to come down, *now!*" My voice suddenly had become more assertive. I was now giving what I quickly learned was the mom stare to Jake, who was continuing to frantically bang on the bubble and laugh.

"Down here now!" I shouted, as I held strong eye contact with him. A few seconds later, Jake flew out from the slide. His face was frowning, and he looked sad.

"I don't want to go home; I want to stay here!" he screamed. I desperately tried to explain to a recently turned five-year-old, whose developmental age was more two, that his time had run out at Chuck E. Cheese. Jake had no concept of time and struggled with transition. Jake had just turned five a few days into the adoption process.

We started to pack up our belongings to walk out of Chuck E. Cheese. Jake let out a loud shriek and fell to the floor. David and I were not used to hearing a child scream and certainly not a child who belonged to us. It was so loud.

"No! No! I don't want to leave! Leave me alone! I don't want to go home!" After attempting to get down to eye level and follow all the wonderful parenting tools we had studied, we quickly realized that Jake could not hear us over his loud screaming. Everyone in Chuck E. Cheese seemed to be staring at us.

David made a quick decision to pick Jake up, and he took him out to the parking lot. After crying for around thirty minutes, Jake ended his meltdown as quickly as it had started, and he was silent. After driving up to Jessica's foster home, I jumped out of the truck to open the door for Jessica. She was quiet and looked upset.

"What's wrong, Jessica? Are you okay?" I felt perplexed that she looked so upset after seeing her enjoy herself at Chuck E. Cheese. Her head hung low as she got out of the car.

"I peed myself." Tears started to fill her eyes. I suddenly felt a wave of embarrassment as I saw that her bib overalls were soaking wet. How had we not thought to take two young children of five and six for a bathroom break! *How am I going to explain this to her foster mom?* I thought. Thankfully, Jessica's foster mom seemed to be very understanding.

She smiled and said, "It will be one of many mistakes you will make as new parents."

As I returned to the truck, I took a deep breath. My brother had always told me how tough parenting was. *This certainly is not for the fainthearted!* I thought. David and I were still learning how to transition from being a couple to parents, and we only had ten days from meeting our children to learn to be parents before they officially moved in with us and said good-bye to their foster parents.

Over the next couple of months, our family began to bond as we spent many days going out as a family and visiting zoos, water parks, the mountains and toy shops. We had lost out on the early years of their lives and we had so much time to make up. Jake was five and Jessica was six when they first came to live with us. It felt wonderful to be called Mom.

When they fell asleep at night, David and I often caught a few minutes to watch them sleep. All the meltdowns seemed insignificant when we watched them sleep peacefully. They had experienced so much loss and pain in their first five years of life.

I felt so blessed and grateful that I had found a purpose to my life. I was thankful that I had made the decision to live rather than to give up and end my life. Life had not turned out the way I had planned. Miraculously, David and I, among all the people we could have met, had found each other. Some would say that, in itself, was a miracle or a match made in heaven.

Looking back on all that happened in our lives, David and I can now see clearly how God was at work, even during our darkest moments when we believed that God had forgotten about us.

Even before I met David at college, God showed me how He had begun His work behind the scenes. While I was on break in southern England, I had felt led to ask a visiting preacher about Canada. He had not ever mentioned Canada, and most of his missions were carried out in Israel. Something seemed to be drawing my attention to Canada.

The visiting preacher arranged my first visit to Canada, and a few years later I returned with David. Even though we returned to the United Kingdom to take a pastorate, the urge to move to Canada did not leave us and as the days, weeks and months went by, the urge to live and work in Canada kept getting stronger.

As David and I continued to look for a solution to our issue and while I worried about my marriage ending, God was at work behind the scenes preparing us to meet our son and daughter.

Not knowing anything about our future children and not even being aware that we would eventually go down the adoption route, David and I immigrated to Canada in May 2008, which we later found out was about five months after Jessica was born. We worked in a small rural oil and gas town of twelve thousand people until 2011 when again we felt a strong urge to relocate to a bigger city in Canada.

Our children were born and placed into foster care in July 2010. Around 2011, the children had ceased all contact with their birth mom, and it seemed they were heading for the adoption path. In 2012, David and I decided that we were going to pursue the adoption route. A plan behind the scenes was coming together that neither David nor I was aware of. All we could see were the struggles and challenges we had faced.

In May 2014, our children officially became members of our family and although there have been many challenges along the way, David and I feel so blessed. Our daughter has similar attributes and characteristics that I do, and my son has traits like David's. God chose our children, and we feel they are a perfect match.

Being Dad *(David's Perspective)*
Since the children were with us, I had left the forensic mental health system and taken paternity leave for eight months. During this time, I was privileged to receive 80 percent of my monthly income through employment insurance. So, during this amazing time off, I was able to take Jake and Jessica into the heart of the Canadian Rockies. We went there about four times each week, while Rachel was working. It only took just over an hour to get to the town nestled in the Canadian Rockies. We avoided the highway, as it was too fast and busy. Besides, we saw more coyotes on the old road, as it wound through Native American land.

At around 9:00 a.m. on our trips to the Canadian Rockies, Jake and Jessica would throw rocks into the water at the lakes up in the mountains. By 11:30 a.m., we were eating McDonald's as we traveled an old highway back to a small town where we could watch the trains really close up and throw rocks into the river. Later, we would head back to the city so that in the afternoon, we were able to go to the park if the weather was good.

So here I was, a dad. I had no idea that my life would take the shape that it did. I had so many preconceived ideas, yet we could not conceive! And now, as strange as it felt at times, Jake and Jessica were our children.

They started off calling us "Rachel" and "David." Then it was "Daddy David" and "Mommy Rachel." After a couple of weeks, it was just "Mom and Dad."

There was so much to learn about being a parent, and there still is. Every day, I am faced with new challenges, and there is no infallible textbook or guide to lead us through the process of this role of parenthood. There is so much else to talk about, but that is truly another book in itself.

Seed for Thought
"I will give you hidden treasures, riches stored in secret places, so that you may know that I am the Lord, the God of Israel, who summons you by name" (Isaiah 45:3).

CHAPTER FIFTEEN

Financially Blessed and Restored

"Success is 99 percent failure." —Soichiro Honda

Amazingly, God also financially blessed us. After spending huge amounts of money on counseling, Botox and psychologists, God restored every penny and more. We later found out that the Canadian city we had located to was the only place in Canada, and likely one of the few places in the world, that financially supported our children until the children turned eighteen years old. Each month from the time the children were placed in our care, they paid a support check into our account to help us with raising our children.

God has always supplied all our needs and fully restored what we had lost. When David left the Christian ministry because of the stress of our vaginismus, God already had a job lined up and it was at double the wage he had earned as a pastor. God continued to bless us.

After five years of having the children live with us, both David and I felt that God wanted us to return to be near our families in the United Kingdom. The children needed extended family, such as cousins, uncles, aunts, grandmas and grandads, and Jake required specialized interventions that we knew would be available in the UK.

One evening, David and I were thinking about the prospect of placing our home on the market. We still had not secured jobs, had not figured out where we would live, and had no plans in place. I was becoming quite stressed, as I was constantly trying to plan out a timeline on paper that would work to transition all our family, our two cats and an Alaskan malamute sled dog we had just accidently rescued from a nearby shelter. Tika was the only dog that had been left at the shelter over the Christmas period. I had visited the shelter on December 22 with my daughter to read to the animals and when we arrived, we were informed that all the animals had been fostered out over the Christmas period. However, Tika had not been deemed suitable to be placed in a home due to her extreme fear of human contact and had been deemed unadoptable because she had been in the shelter over four months.

I remembered the day well.

"What's happening with this dog?" I asked as I saw a dog sitting in its crate alone.

"Oh, she is the only dog we cannot foster out, as she doesn't trust humans due to being so badly abused."

I learned the owner of the shelter had attempted to take her to her house but had to return her back to the shelter because she could not settle.

After talking with the shelter manager and with approval from the upper rescue management, David and I decided to open our home to Tika over the Christmas period. For six months I fed her by spoon, and she hid in our bathroom. She could not even be taken for walks due to her extreme fear of the outside world. She was not house trained and would have accidents on many occasions. When we did try to take her out into the garden, she would heavily pant and scrape at the door to go back inside.

As I continued to research flights for our family and pets to the UK, I worried about whether the move would set her back, but everything in me knew I could not abandon her now. She had just started to eat out of a bowl and had begun to allow us to take her for short walks; I could not send her back to the shelter. David was listening to his music in the kitchen, and I was sitting in the family room trying to plan out the next twelve months.

"Hey, Rachel, what do you think about calling Arlene and asking for an appraisal on our house? I could call her tomorrow."

I looked at David as if he had lost his mind. It was February, the middle of winter, with heavy snow on the ground and forty-below-zero weather.

"Are you serious? Who would want to buy a house in the middle of nowhere in a small oil and gas town where there is barely any work, in the middle of winter?" Strangely, David and I had returned to this middle of nowhere oil and gas town for a second time round after we had adopted our children. After adopting our children, the small town seemed better suited to raising our children for the younger years of their lives.

David ignored my sane comments and continued with his crazy plan.

"I'm just going to test the water, see what she comes back with. I just think we need to get the ball rolling. I know you said June, but something tells me we should be trying to sell now," David said insistently.

The next day, David collected me from work and drove me to the real estate office to see Arlene. She had been in the business for over forty years, so she knew her market well.

"Well, I'm afraid you are really choosing the wrong time to sell, guys. I think you should wait a few months. Right now, you would be lucky to get more than $218,000 US dollars for your house." She then proceeded to show us all the houses that had sat on the market for over a year.

"This is what you are up against, guys. This one has way more to offer than your house, and it hasn't moved, and its selling price is way cheaper than what you are expecting."

I knew that in order to move back to the United Kingdom, we needed to sell our house for $238,000, so $218,000 was not going to work.

"I think we should list it for $254,000," I said boldly. Arlene let out a little chuckle.

"It would be a miracle if it sold for that price, and if you want to move soon, you really would be holding up your plans for possibly a year to sell for that price."

I replied, "Well, we believe that if the man upstairs wants us to move, then it will sell for what we need, which is a minimum of $238,000."

With that, our house was placed on the market the following Monday. It was February and the middle of winter with a windchill of minus forty degrees. Our real estate adviser said that most people did not want to move or search for houses in the middle of winter, especially in an isolated town in Canada! By the next day we had an offer for $238,000 US dollars. Both David and I suddenly realized that we now needed to act fast because the new owners wanted to move into the house in March.

"What are we going to do, Dave? We won't have anywhere to live!" I frantically started pricing Airbnb and hotels and it was coming to thousands of dollars. After praying about our situation, I had the thought to go back to the buyers and offer them our gym equipment if they would allow us to remain in our house until the end of April, which they agreed to do, saving us a lot of money.

Meanwhile, my parents were searching for a rental that would suit our family, which was proving difficult with two cats and a big Alaskan malamute.

After many months of trying to work out a plan to get to the United Kingdom, it seemed that at the last minute everything began to fall into place. The animals were all booked on the same flight as us, a rental house in Canada became available for three weeks for our family, and my parents found a house to rent in the United Kingdom that would allow our two cats, Alaskan malamute and our two children. Now all that was left was to find the right house to buy.

David and I visited a mortgage lender about finding a house. We had been advised by many people that it was unlikely that we had any chance of getting a house for a few years due to our lack of credit history in the United Kingdom after living eleven years in Canada. We had only just secured jobs and started working in the UK a few months before, so most people found our dreams of purchasing a house in the UK unreasonable. It did not stop me from looking at houses and putting in my requests to God about what our family required.

"This one is nice, David. It's a stand-alone, has a beautiful garden and is right next to where the children go to school. This house would be perfect!"

David sometimes had to bring me back from dreamland, but this time I was adamant that we needed this house. David disagreed that we could afford the house but every other house we viewed did not seem to meet our needs as a family. Our son was extremely noisy and there was no way we could have anything but a single-family home. It wasn't a want. It was a need.

"Rachel, there is no way we can afford that house! We need to look at houses that are much more affordable. I do not think we will be getting a house for a long time, Rachel! They won't even let us buy an iPhone if we haven't been in the country for three years. What makes you think we can buy a house?"

After two months of being back in the UK, we secured a house, and it was the single-family home we had wanted. We had a six-month rental lease that had to be paid before we moved. Thankfully, because there ended up being a few issues with land boundaries, we ended up having the moving date stalled until December, which ended up being available to us at the time our six-month rental agreement was up.

Everything that happened in our lives happened for a reason, even the pain and suffering we experienced. David and I could so easily have given up on our marriage. No one would have blamed us for giving up, and it would have been so easy to have just annulled our marriage and separated, rather than taking the long journey of fighting our issue. Now, looking back, I see how many blessings David and I would have missed out on.

Even when God does not seem to be present and the heavens seem deathly silent, He is always there. Sometimes His plans do not fit your plans, and you can only see a small part of the picture that He sees. Because you cannot see the bigger picture, you start to question the reasons why certain situations are occurring, or why it seems that you were overlooked or lost out on something that you had wanted.

But when the time comes for God to reveal His plans, you will realize that God has taken all the broken pieces of your life that seemed unable to be fixed and created a unique masterpiece that is more magnificent than you could ever have imagined. God knows your situation. He has not forgotten you and He sees your tears and hears your pleas. He also knows all your strengths, your weaknesses and the areas of your life that are preventing you from being the best version of you.

It is time to take on the fight and not give up hope. The time will come when your pain ends, the problem will be overcome and your love for each other will become unbreakable. At that wonderful time, the beautiful masterpiece that He has created you both to be will shine like the stars.

Seed for Thought

"I prayed for this child, and the Lord has granted me what I asked of him" (First Samuel 1:27).

CHAPTER SIXTEEN

Bringing Down the Walls

"When everything seems to be going against you, remember that the airplane takes off against the wind, not with it." —Henry Ford

We circled the wilderness battling vaginismus for around eleven years, and when the moment came when we achieved sexual intercourse, I remember crying tears of pure joy. I remember the shock and the smile of joy that covered David's face. It is a memory of pure happiness that I will treasure forever. I no longer experienced the familiar pain, frustration and tears of shame. I remember when David told me that he was completely inside of me and how surprised I was, as I felt no pain. Like in the book of Joshua where the Israelites finally saw the walls of Jericho fall flat, finally my Jericho walls had crashed to the ground after years of waiting. In the book of Joshua, God promised the Israelites that the city of Jericho would be their inheritance. God gave them a promise that seemed utterly impossible. The book of Joshua describes the walls of Jericho as tough and thick, and they reached high up into the skies. These were not thin walls that would be easy to smash down. When the Israelites looked at these walls with their human eyes, quite understandably they saw their promised inheritance and considered it to be an impossibility. Here they were, in a land called Canaan, full of giants and warriors, and they were still roaming aimlessly in the wilderness. Although God had promised them their victory, the Israelites did not see that. All that they saw was the obstacle that stood in the way of their promise of claiming the city of Jericho.

If you are still waiting on God's promise for your Jericho to be defeated, a scripture that you must claim is Joshua 6:2 "***See,*** I ***have*** delivered Jericho into your hands, along with its king and its fighting men." This scripture shows that God has ***already*** given you your victory." Part of my victory over vaginismus involved taking a step of faith and traveling to New Hampshire, where I would receive Botox. Negative thoughts flooded my mind of what could go wrong and what would happen if it failed. I realized that there were many giants in my life that had to be slain before I could even get near defeating my Jericho, which was the vaginismus that had dominated my life for years and kept me in bondage. If I were to truly experience freedom like the Israelites, I had to face up to the many phobias and anxieties that were governing my life. In particular, I had to first of all face my fear of death and phobias around taking medications head on.

For the Israelites, looking at claiming Jericho from a human perspective seemed impossible. It took faith and obedience in God for them to be victorious. Like you and me, the Israelites had to become tired of remaining stuck in the wilderness and feeling defeated in order to trust God's ways of defeating the walls that stood in the way of them claiming Jericho. If we are not sick of where we are, then we will go nowhere. Overcoming big challenges like vaginismus often involves many other fights and tests that we must complete *before* the walls of our Jericho can come crashing down and bring us victory.

The book of Joshua is all about God testing our faith and our obedience to Him. God wants His people to get to a point of trusting Him, even when it does not make sense or when it seems to be unfair. God did not instruct the Israelites to immediately attack the walls. Instead, He told them to quietly circle the walls over a seven-day period and to walk without talking and wait until the day that He would tell them to shout and claim their victory. The book of Joshua clearly shows there was a period of waiting, obeying and trusting. God was teaching the Israelites not to fix their eyes on the problem they were facing, but to fix their eyes on what He had promised to them. "But the righteous will live by his faith" (Habakkuk 2:4b). After I had received the Botox treatment, I expected to have sex by my wedding anniversary, which was around ten days after my procedure. After eleven years of crying myself to sleep on every past anniversary, I was excited that my next wedding anniversary would be different. However, when my anniversary arrived, I was left feeling disappointed, angry and confused. I had stepped out in faith for the treatment and I had faced my giant phobias, yet the vaginismus still did not seem to have been defeated. As I sat there feeling defeated, I did not realize that my victory was closer than I had expected. I was so close, but all that I could see were the walls facing me that seemed even more impossible to break through after receiving a treatment that I had regarded to be the absolute solution. When we expect a breakthrough, and it does not happen like we expect it to, our faith is put to the test. Unbeknownst to me, my victory was only a few weeks away.

The book of Joshua shows that God instructed the Israelites to *continue circling the walls of Jericho while focusing on the promise* that the city of Jericho would be theirs. They were instructed to do this over seven days and to remain silently confident. It wasn't an immediate thing. A few weeks later, I had my breakthrough after achieving sexual intimacy, and the wall had gone. Vaginismus was finally resolved. After years of circling my Jericho, I had perceived my anticipated victory very differently than what had actually occurred. Whenever breakthrough occurs, we then have a healing process. When someone goes through the healing process after an intense battle, they are often left with certain scars that are not visible to everyone else. Victory truly is a magical moment. But vaginismus had left many scars that etched themselves into my being, as a reminder of the battle that I had overcome. In this context, vaginismus is a condition that will always be a part of who I am. This is not said in a negative way. I am simply keeping things real. Like women who have overcome breast cancer, the fight will always be a part of them, and they will never forget.

After achieving the ability to have sex, we realized that a lot of healing had to take place in our marriage before we could freely enjoy sexual intimacy. Years of feeling rejected and repulsed at sex, years of withdrawing from each other to survive, and years of experiencing nothing but excruciating pain are not memories that just disappear overnight. It has taken ongoing work by both of us over many years to build new levels of trust and patience with each other and to heal from the wounds that vaginismus left behind. But like any other marriage, trials come and go. Marriage can only be truly successful if both partners are willing to work together in order to overcome the trials that face them. Our story clearly proves that marriages that seem beyond the possibility of repair can survive and thrive if both partners are truly committed. I can promise you that the victory is well worth the waiting and the fight. After twenty-one years of marriage, David and I have no regrets about our fight to save our marriage. Battling vaginismus has taught us to take nothing in life for granted and to make every second together count.

Being content in a marriage is something that is unique for everyone. Our contentment is that we have realized that having sexual intercourse is not something that is a must in our relationship. Although we can achieve sex now, it is not something that our relationship must depend upon in order to function at its best potential. It is a gift that we have. But if it were taken away from us again, our marriage would not fall apart. Vaginismus has allowed us to be content in so many other ways, rather than just relying on sexual fulfilment to feel content with our marriage. It is not the ability to engage in sexual intercourse that defines our marriage and commitment to each other. Society puts so much emphasis on sex that it places immense pressure on couples to feel that marriages cannot thrive without it. Marriage can thrive without sex being the main cornerstone. Many relationships survive without sex, or little sex, and are strong and fulfilling. Some couples choose to remain asexual and others do not have the privilege of a sexual relationship (due to medical illness). Many marriages in these circumstances still thrive. These marriages and partnerships are often special and unique because the partners' love for each other goes beyond the fulfilment of sexual expectations that *must be met*. It is a love that becomes truly unbroken and unconditional and survives through whatever season of life they are facing.

No one knows what other battles we will be called to face in this lifetime. But those couples who have achieved unbroken love can feel secure in the knowledge that whatever trial they face will be faced together. In whatever part of the journey you find yourself, remember the promise that God has given to you in Joshua 6:2, "**See** I **have** delivered Jericho into your hands". Again, He has **already** given you your victory! Although you may still be circling those walls, they will come crashing down in the course of time. I cannot promise you that it will be tomorrow, next month or two years from now. Only God knows the date of your victory. All I know is that if you keep walking around your walls and thanking God for His promise, your victory will come. In Hebrews 12:2-3 it says, "Let us fix our eyes on Jesus, the author and perfecter of our faith, who for the joy set before him endured the cross, scorning its shame, and sat down at the right hand of the throne of God. Consider him who endured such opposition from sinful men, so that you will not grow weary and lose heart." God instructs us to shout our victory on the day that breakthrough comes (Joshua 6:10). Then He promises that the walls will fall flat (Joshua 6:20). Today, if you remember nothing else, remember that you are fighting from a place of victory and not from a place of failure. You may *think* differently, and you may *feel* differently, but the battle has not ended until you experience the victory *that you have been promised*.

Seed for Thought
"Be strong and courageous. Do not be terrified; and do not be discouraged, for the Lord your God will be with you wherever you go" (Joshua 1:9b).

A Letter to the Reader

This book was begun during one of the most difficult times of my life, a time I will remember as being painful. However, twenty years later, I look back on this time and I thank God that He sent me through this difficult time, as I believe that it enabled me to grow into the person I have become today. Without this experience, I do not believe I would have the ability to undertake the role of helping other individuals who are experiencing mental health or psychological stress. If life had been perfect and I had never experienced pain, how could I possibly even begin to know how to try to stand in the shoes of another?

As you know, David and I never got to be the parents of a biological child. Instead, we now believe that God set us both aside for a much bigger challenge of adoption. After completing the training and the interviews, David and I finally became parents to two wonderful children who were ages five and six when they came to live with us. They had been living in foster care for four and half years and were biological siblings. Sadly, after they were removed from their birth mom, they were placed in separate foster homes. Once David and I agreed to become their parents, they were then placed together with us in their forever home. We are a family who have all fought different battles and experienced different pain.

I know that sometimes it can be difficult to share such private pain with others. It took over twelve years for this book to be written, as part of me battled with God about sharing such private pain with others. However, I hope and pray that it will bring some comfort to you to know that you are never alone.

Life never turned out how I expected it to. But looking back on the journey David and I had to take to get to the place where we are now,

I can honestly say that I do not regret or wish away any of the years of pain I experienced. When I first got married, the life I had planned out was idealistic and I was naïve in many ways and had a lot to learn. The experience of living eleven years with vaginismus was an experience I would never want to repeat, but I would if it meant that I had the life I am living now.

To all of you who are still in that place of despair, please do not give up hope. Know that even though you may feel alone, you are never alone. It might sometimes feel like God has forgotten about you or cannot hear your cries, but know that He can hear you and He has not forgotten you. Even though where you are right now is tough, you are right where you need to be. You are in the palm of His hand, and during the tough times, He is carrying you through.

I know you might not see any hope right now, and some of you will be contemplating suicide because you feel you cannot take another day of pain. It is tough to see the light at the end of the tunnel, especially when you are alone in the middle of the dark. It is difficult to believe that the light will eventually arrive, especially when you cannot see it and you have never walked this journey before.

That day will come when life feels better again. It might not be tomorrow, this week or even next year, but know that it will come when the timing is right.

Hold on to God's promise, "I will never leave you or forsake you," in Deuteronomy 31:6. You are not in this storm alone; He is always with you, even when you cannot see or hear Him. Take one step at a time, put one foot in front of the other, and do not place high expectations on yourself that you cannot meet.

Keep moving forward and don't give up, and you will eventually meet the joy of the morning.

Seed for Thought
"Because of the Lord's great love we are not consumed, for his compassions never fail. They are new every morning; great is your faithfulness" (Lamentations 3:22–23).

Appendix 1

Template Letters for Family Doctor/Spiritual Leaders

In this section you will find a letter that can be copied or adapted that you can hand to a healthcare professional or your spiritual leader with the hope that it will allow you to seek help in a less threatening manner. I know how painful and exhausting it can be trying to explain to healthcare professionals what you are going through, so this is my gift to you.

Dear Healthcare Professional,

The pain feels like knives, burning and searing pain that is so bad I must tell him to stop. Every time we try to have sex, it feels like we are continually hitting a brick wall. It does not matter how many attempts he has made at trying to enter me, or how much I try and relax, it does not work!

I have a condition known as vaginismus, which comes under the term Genito Pelvic Pain/Penetration Disorder as defined by the DSM-5.

As a vaginismus patient, I would ask that when I visit your office, you are aware that you are probably the very first person I have disclosed my condition to. I am most likely in the midst of a crisis because I am in fear of losing my partner. I most definitely will be feeling embarrassed and extremely vulnerable too.

I do not have the unrealistic expectation that you will have expert knowledge about vaginismus. But I would like to ask that you try to place yourself in my situation and understand how difficult this disclosure is for me. Simply taking the time to seek out someone you can refer me to would be great as well.

Please do not label me with a diagnosis of vaginismus until you have ruled out every other possible physical cause. I am only going to keep on hounding you for answers if you do not rule out physical causes for my pain, before labeling me as having vaginismus. Ruling out other physiological causes immediately allows me to then focus on managing my sexual pain disorder, rather than wasting time trying to seek out other reasons for my pain. It also shows me that you have taken my pain seriously. Provide information on the vast selection of dilators that are available to me and someone who can provide me with direction on how to use them correctly.

Maybe a nurse in your practice could take an interest in teaching dilation techniques and how and when to use them. I also need someone to coach me, for however long it takes for me to overcome my disorder. I need my doctor to be committed to my success and to not give up hope when I fail to reach my goals. Have a plan if I fail the dilation treatment, rather than just giving up on me. Maybe my vaginismus is more severe than you first anticipated. Research the Lamont Scale so you can identify the severity of my vaginismus—am I a stage one or a stage five? Know what level of the disorder you are dealing with.

Providing some useful websites for me to visit for ongoing advice and social support can also help. Remember, this condition isolates many women and many, like me, find they have no one to confide in—they need emotional support. Referral to a psychologist for cognitive behavioral therapy (CBT) or dialectical behavioral therapy (DBT) and mindfulness techniques are other possibilities to consider. Consider the causes of the sexual pain disorder and refer accordingly. If a victim of trauma or rape, then a referral to a sexual abuse or rape counselor may be one of the referrals you might consider.

Women from strict religious upbringings may require a counselor sensitive to women with sexual pain disorders who need to be re-educated about their negative belief system toward sex. It is vitally important that women still have the ongoing support of their doctor, so that the physiological component of their sexual pain can be addressed alongside the other therapy. Some women may present with a condition so severe that no amount of counseling or dilation therapy is going to be effective. These women may require further assessment for Botox treatment in addition to dilation therapy.

I hope that my recommendations and my letter to you have provided some, if only a small, insight into managing a patient with vaginismus. This condition requires more publicity and more acceptance as being a condition that is serious and requires ongoing support.

Often you are the first point of contact for the woman or for the couple, which is why your role in dealing with vaginismus is so important. The effects of vaginismus on a person's mental health should not be underestimated. Always be vigilant for suicidal ideation or intent, as many women will often question their existence as a woman, which can lead to depression and suicidal intent.

Sincerely,

Dear Pastor and Counselors,

I have a condition known as vaginismus, which comes under the term Genito Pelvic Pain/Penetration Disorder as defined by the DSM-5.

The pain feels like knives, burning and searing pain that is so bad that I have to tell him to stop. Every time that we try and have sex, it feels like we are continually hitting a brick wall. It does not matter how many attempts he has made at trying to enter me, or how much I try and relax—it does not work!

I had no idea what to expect when I entered my marriage, and that is the truth. Everyone *assumed* that we already knew what we needed to know. Looking back now, I can clearly see that I was not adequately prepared, and I was still stuck in the mind-set that sex was wrong and forbidden. I need to hear from the church leaders that sex is normal and not dirty. I need sex to be normalized. I have carried negative beliefs surrounding sex into my relationship unnecessarily, and it almost destroyed my marriage before it had even begun. I have struggled to move from the transition of sex being forbidden to sex suddenly being acceptable.

    I am sitting in your office seeking help, as I am utterly broken, and I do not know how we can fix this. I need prayer for myself and my partner, and I need to be taken seriously. Please do not undermine us, judge us or laugh at and ridicule us. Sadly, this has happened to other women who have approached their church leadership for help. If we are confiding in you, it is because we are at a point of crisis. This condition tears marriages apart before they even start, and we do not want our marriage to be destroyed, so please do not turn us away. We may need a lot more of your time and support, and I may cry a lot. My partner may come across angry because he does not know what to do and who to speak to.

    I have been informed that I need to use dilators and may need Botox treatment, and often I need to have some cognitive behavioral therapy, which works on changing my thoughts, feelings and behaviors. The church can help by offering the spiritual support I need and praying for me and letting me know that sex is a beautiful act and not something to be ashamed of. Let me know I am not less of a person because I have this condition. Please do not overlook me for working in the church or singing in the worship band. I need things in church to carry on as normal, and I need to feel accepted.

Sincerely,

Appendix 2

Quotations of Encouragement

"You begin to fly when you let go of self-limiting beliefs and allow your mind and aspirations to rise to greater heights." —Brian Tracy

"Do not limit yourself. Many people limit themselves to what they think they can do. You can go as far as your mind lets you. What you believe, remember, you can achieve." —Mary Kay Ash

"If you accept a limiting belief, then it will become a truth for you." —Louise Hay

"Do the uncomfortable. Become comfortable with these acts. Prove to yourself that your limiting beliefs die a quick death if you will simply do what you feel uncomfortable doing." —Darren Rowse

"Remember: we all get what we tolerate. So stop tolerating excuses within yourself, limiting beliefs of the past, or half-assed or fearful states." —Tony Robbins

"Our limitations and success will be based, most often, on our own expectations for ourselves. What the mind dwells upon, the body acts upon." —Denis Waitley

"Start by doing what's necessary; then do what's possible; and suddenly you are doing the impossible." —Francis of Assisi

"Success is to be measured not so much by the position that one has reached in life as by the obstacles which he has overcome." —Booker T. Washington

"Success is 99 percent failure." —Soichiro Honda

"Turn your wounds into wisdom." —Oprah Winfrey

"I can't change the direction of the wind, but I can adjust my sails to always reach my destination." —Jimmy Dean

"You are the one that possesses the keys to your being. You carry the passport to your own happiness." —Diane von Furstenberg

"Complexity is the enemy of execution." —Tony Robbins

"Get clear on what you really want and where you really are." —Tony Robbins

"Knowing what must be done does away with fear." —Rosa Parks

"Power is not given to you. You have to take it." —Beyoncé Knowles Carter

"The difference between successful people and others is how long they spend feeling sorry for themselves." —Barbara Corcoran

"I'd rather regret the things I've done than regret the things I haven't done." —Lucille Ball

"If you want to take the island, then burn the boats." —Tony Robbins

"If you don't risk anything, you risk even more." —Erica Jong

"Step out of the history that is holding you back. Step into the new story you are willing to create." —Oprah Winfrey

"What you do makes a difference, and you have to decide what kind of difference you want to make." —Jane Goodall

"Above all, be the heroine of your life, not the victim." —Nora Ephron

"You should treat your marriage like a business that you wouldn't want to fail." —Lisa Ling

"Intimacy is not purely physical; it is the act of connecting with someone so deeply, you feel like you can see into their soul." —Author unknown

"The Christian life is not a constant high. I have moments of deep discouragement. I have to go to God in prayer with tears in my eyes and say, 'Oh God, forgive me' or 'Help me.'" —Billy Graham

"Worry does not empty tomorrow of its sorrow, it empties today of its strength." —Corrie ten Boom

"Be brave. God gives his hardest battles to his bravest soldiers." —Author Unknown

"God never said that the journey would be easy. But He did say that the arrival would be worthwhile." —Max Lucado

"Never be afraid to trust an unknown future to a known God." —Corrie ten Boom

"Earth's troubles fade in the light of heaven's hope." —Billy Graham

"God is always doing 10,000 things in your life, and you may be aware of three of them." —John Piper

"When you understand that life is a test, you realize that nothing is insignificant in your life." —Rick Warren